Best
Regards

Naga
Hendricks
Sept. 2008

LEAVING EUROPE

LEAVING EUROPE

A Cross-Cultural Memoir

MONIQUE HENDRICKS

Xlibris

Copyright © 2006 by Monique Hendricks

Cover Photograph by Adam Hendricks
Author Photograph by Adam Hendricks

Library of Congress Control Number:		2006905890
ISBN:	Hardcover	1-4257-2354-3
	Softcover	1-4257-2353-5

All rights reserved. No part of this book may be reproduced or transmitted in any form or by any means, electronic or mechanical, including photocopying, recording, or by any information storage and retrieval system, without permission in writing from the copyright owner.

This book was printed in the United States of America.

To order additional copies of this book, contact:
Xlibris Corporation
1-888-795-4274
www.Xlibris.com
Orders@Xlibris.com

This book is dedicated to my mother, Claude,
a pioneer in her own right and a continuing source of inspiration.

Acknowledgments

I am grateful to Katrijn de Graef, who planted the seed one warm summer's night in June 2003, while we were driving to Bice's for a fine Italian meal. Thank you also to my dear friend Diane Hooper who, for the past eight years, has supported every one of my whims as we walked, talked and ate our way out of trouble. Most sincere thanks to Wendy Ashman, my English friend and very own editor (though she might have rued the day she volunteered to read my manuscript when Chapter One landed on her desk at Mulberry Lodge). And, of course, this book would never have seen the light of day if it weren't for the love and encouragement of the three men in my life: Frank, Adam, Stewart.

CONTENTS

Chapter	1	SWITZERLAND	13
	2	ENGLAND	63
	3	SWITZERLAND	73
	4	GERMANY	97
	5	BELGIUM	109
	6	USA	117
	7	ICELAND	123
	8	USA	135
	9	BELGIUM	139
	10	SWITZERLAND	145

Plus ça change, plus c'est la même chose.

Chapter One: SWITZERLAND

I remember being loved as a child. I also remember telling my father at eighteen: *"J'en ai marre! Je m'en vais."* ("I'm fed up! I'm leaving.") And so I did, embarking on what would become a lifelong quest for greener pastures, and the apparent need to keep a large body of water—or at least a border—between my father and me.

* * *

The unexamined life is not worth living, Socrates warned. I like that saying. I have it written down on several scraps of paper lying around the house, as a reminder.

I was born in November 1951 in a hospital in Berne, Switzerland, where my parents, both physicians, had relocated from their respective hometowns, Neuchâtel in my father's case, Lausanne in my mother's. Whenever I think of my childhood, which was quite happy, memories of food lurk not far behind. A summer vacation in Normandy when I was very young is associated with an oversize, freshly baked *tarte aux abricots* carried by an older woman on the beach in the late afternoon. My father recalled with amusement that he brought me to a *pâtisserie* in Lucerne once after visiting a museum, and when he asked what I wanted I timidly pointed at the display and said, *"Une tartelette aux pruneaux, s'il te plaît."* ("A plum tartlet, please.") When my parents shipped me off to an all-girl Catholic school in Lausanne at age fifteen (to save me from boys), I was devastated but quickly consoled myself with visits to the local *boulangerie* where I would make my selection, to be savored in my room later, alone.

My mother was, and still is, a wonderful cook. At ninety, living by herself in a house overlooking Lake Geneva, she continues to bring joy to young and old alike—neighbors, friends, relatives who delight in her company as well as her culinary talents. To this day, when I plan a visit to Maman in Lausanne, her first question, before I've even gotten on the plane, is always, *"Qu'est-ce que tu veux manger?"* ("What do you want to eat?") Detailed menus of past meals or foods yet to be prepared are often discussed in our weekly phone conversations. I don't consider myself a particularly good cook, but I make up for it by reveling in the presentation of the food I serve. One of the reasons I love going to see French movies is that I know there will be at least one scene centering around food in each film.

My father, proud owner of a Kodak 8mm movie camera in the fifties, enjoyed making black-and-white movies of his family, especially when we went on holiday, which was often. Papa loved Italy—its churches, museums, Roman ruins, frescoes, mosaics, antique shops, gastronomy, warm climate, breathtaking scenery. By the time I was ten I think I had seen every historically significant monument in that country. At Easter, we drove to Ticino, the Italian part of Switzerland, and stayed at a small bungalow on Lake Lugano that my parents rented from a Swiss German couple. The lakeside property came with a dog—an old, black Scottish terrier named Ruggeli—and a row boat. My brother and I would take the boat and oar our way across the lake to Caslano, pretending to be smugglers (all we ever smuggled from the other side was driftwood for the fireplace). Papa regularly took us in his Citroën to Ponte Tresa or Varese in Italy, where he went looking for antiques. I hated going into those dusty shops crammed with old furniture, and swore that when I grew up, my apartment would look nothing like my parents' with its Louis Seize armchairs, Greek icons, ornate chandeliers and statues of the Virgin Mary.

Those holidays in Ticino were memorable. Since we spent every Easter there, my mother would organize an egg hunt for my brother and me which took us up and down the terraced flower beds, among the forsythias, around the *saule pleureur* (weeping willow) whose branches fell into the water. Poor old Ruggeli tried to keep up with us, but inevitably tired himself out trudging up and down the garden steps behind us; in the end he would simply plop down somewhere and wait for us to return, baskets full, hoping that a few chocolate eggs would somehow roll out and find their way into his mouth. Over the years I tried to duplicate those egg hunts for my children, but they were never as spectacular as my mother's because we didn't live in such a beautiful setting. From Carabietta, we would take trips to a different part of Italy each spring, and most summers as well: Venice,

Milan, Florence, Genoa, Pisa, Siena, Rome, Naples, Sicily. Growing up I knew Italy much better than my own country. The downside? I was dragged through so many arches, steeples and archaeological sites that I developed an aversion to them. The best holidays were those spent in such places as Ischia, where my parents rented a villa surrounded by pine trees, not too far from the beach and the *gelateria*. The promise of a scoop of pistachio or lemon ice-cream made up for all those visits to so-called cultural institutions. Another summer we stayed at a breezy house in Cervia near Rimini, on the Adriatic Coast, and the fig tree in the garden held much more fascination for me than the nearby mosaics of Ravenna.

In 1963 my father developed tuberculosis. My mother diagnosed it correctly, but Papa told her:

"You're mad! People don't get TB at the age of forty-seven."

Every morning he woke up with a fever, his pajamas soaked. For two months he suffered from jaundice. Finally, he agreed to consult another doctor. The smear confirmed that his lungs were infected with tubercle bacilli. What he had was an open TB, practically galloping consumption, a highly contagious illness. Yet Papa insisted that we all kiss him morning and night. His physician came to the apartment and said:

"You've got to go to the hospital."

"Out of the question. I'm staying here."

"Then I won't be treating you."

Papa ended up staying at Tiefenau Hospital for six months (during which the apartment was thoroughly disinfected). It was recommended that he convalesce for three months afterwards. He first went to Ticino, then in July and August, the four of us—Papa, Maman, my brother and I—vacationed in Saas Fee, breathing in fresh alpine air. Those weeks spent in the mountains, rather than at the beach, were so pleasant that my father decided he wanted to own a chalet. There ensued a lengthy search for the perfect abode in Valais, and in 1964 my parents found a piece of land in the small village of St. Luc in the Val d'Anniviers where they began to build their chalet. From that time on, holidays were spent in St. Luc, but my parents continued to take me abroad (my older brother was no longer required to come with us). We went to Greece one summer, arriving by ferry from Bari into the harbor of Patras. It was dusk; we had reservations at a hotel in Delphi. The drive up to the mythical site of the Oracle, among olive trees and the amber sky at sunset, remains one of the most surreal moments of my life. Couple that with the huge, delectable peaches my mother picked up from a roadside stand, and you'd think you'd died and gone to heaven.

The following summer my parents took me to Turkey, and that, as I recall, was an unabashed disaster. For me, our brief stay at the luxurious

Istanbul Hilton was the high point of our holiday. Unfortunately, my father wanted to see Cappadocia, so we flew to Ankara, and from there headed for Anatolia with a hired English-speaking driver. I did not react well to the food ingested in the many less than sanitary restaurants we stopped at along the way. The fact that our guide spoke to me occasionally didn't help matters with my father, who viewed our friendly exchanges as fraught with sexual danger. Unthinkable for a man, any man (least of all a Turk) to be "flirting" with his daughter under his very nose!

Turkey was our last family vacation.

My brother JC was typically protective of his little sister. He was a sweet and handsome boy, even-tempered, helpful, sometimes amused by my antics. I looked up to him until I became a teenager. Then things changed.

To the outside world, we looked like a typical family of four. But my parents had already experienced trauma when their first child, born prematurely at six months, died shortly after birth. In those days, doctors didn't have the technology they now possess to save preemies. Her name was Claire and I always wondered how different life would have been had I had a sister. My mother wanted more children, but my father was adamantly against it, so after I was born the shop closed for good.

My mother told me years later that my father favored me. Sitting at the dining room table, he would turn his entire body towards me and pay me a great deal of attention—he cut the meat on my plate well into my teens—leaving my brother to stare at his back. I had no awareness of preferential treatment as a small child, and felt equally loved by both parents.

In 1947 my father had the opportunity to do research at Barnes Hospital in St. Louis. He was told by colleagues that it wouldn't be practical to bring his wife along, let alone the baby—housing was scarce and expensive in post-war America. My parents had very little money to spare. But Papa made it very clear that he expected Maman to accompany him: he would take a mistress in St. Louis if she didn't. Naturally, my mother was torn between staying with her son in Switzerland and following her husband to the US. In the end, it was decided that my one-year-old brother would be left behind, in his paternal grandmother's care. My father sailed on the *Sobieski* from Genoa in June, and Maman followed on the *Queen Mary* from Southampton that October. The decision to leave her infant son behind is one that my mother regretted all her life. At Barnes Hospital, Papa carried out fundamental research on hypertension and renal dialysis with the help of his wife—he didn't want her helping other researchers. The two of them lived in a sparsely furnished room, where Maman cooked supper on a makeshift stove: a Meta camping lamp. Day-old bread was bought at half-price, and occasionally they treated themselves to an entire doughnut, to be split between them.

Despite limited funds, my parents managed to do some sightseeing while they lived in the States, and even attended concerts in New York, St. Louis and San Francisco. Two days after my mother arrived in New York, she and Papa went to Niagara Falls. Between Christmas and New Year's, they drove from St. Louis to Denver with another doctor—divorced, depressed, longing to visit his children there—and skied at Berthoud Pass (elev. 11,300 ft.), named after the Swiss guy who discovered it. In March 1948 they spent two weeks traveling by Greyhound to San Diego, Los Angeles—where they met several professors, one a Nobel prize winner—and San Francisco, stopping in El Paso and Phoenix on the way out, and returning via the Grand Canyon and Santa Fe. To avoid paying for hotels, they slept on the bus. Before Maman sailed back to Europe on the *Queen Elizabeth,* two months ahead of Papa, they visited Washington and Atlantic City.

Grandmaman de Neuchâtel (as we called her) was not my favorite grandmother. Sure, she gave my brother and me tons of chocolate bars at Christmas and for our birthdays. And when, on occasion, we visited her and Grandpapa in Neuchâtel, she would prepare the best *goûter* (mid-afternoon snack): *tranches de tresse au Parfait* (goose liver pâté spread on thin slices of brioche), macaroons, petits fours, assorted *pâtisseries* (my favorite was *caraque,* a tartlet filled with dark chocolate ganache and topped with bright green icing). And I loved browsing through Grandmaman's collection of *Jours de France*—a French magazine filled with pages and pages of elegant women, often princesses and celebrities such as Grace de Monaco, Farah Dibah, Catherine Deneuve, modeling the most exquisite gowns. But Grandmaman de Neuchâtel was not as interesting as Grandmaman de Lausanne, my maternal grandmother. Even though I have no memory of the sort of presents she gave me, her influence was much greater. Grandmaman de Lausanne and her husband, *le colonel divisionnaire,* lived in Lausanne in an old-fashioned apartment on Avenue de Rumine. (We had in our family a peculiar habit of referring to relatives by their addresses rather than their names; thus, going to Rumine meant going to see my maternal grandparents.) The only sunlit rooms were those facing the lake, and the view from there was enchanting. I don't remember what Grandmaman de Lausanne cooked, except for *spaghetti alla bolognese,* which seemed to be her signature dish, and *risotto aux champignons.* According to Maman, her mother was an unusually creative cook, experimenting with various herbs and vegetables, and incorporating mushrooms in many of her dishes. My grandmother loved to pick her own mushrooms, which were plentiful—both the edible and the poisonous kind—in nearby forests. She would pick the ones she knew for sure were edible and put them in one of her coat pockets; the ones she wasn't sure of she would place in another pocket, to be examined at home with the help of her mushroom book collection. She never poisoned anyone that I know of, so her methodology worked. Her husband, very demanding in other aspects of family life, was not so in culinary matters. He loved rice and canned spinach. Whenever my grandmother cooked fresh spinach he complained that it wasn't as succulent as canned spinach. One day Grandmaman and my mother decided to play a trick on him. They cooked fresh spinach, chopped it as finely as they could, added spices and a bit of milk, to imitate the texture of canned spinach, and served it to *le colonel*. He took one bite and voiced his approval with gusto: *"Alors ça, on voit que c'est des épinards en boîte!"* ("Well, this is obviously canned spinach!")

Since I don't associate my maternal grandmother with food, that can't be what drew me to her. I began to realize as I grew older that she was quite eccentric, whereas my paternal grandmother was very much of a conformist. I liked Grandmaman de Lausanne's quirky humor, delivered in self-deprecating fashion, with a shoulder-shrugging chuckle. One Christmas dinner, my brother and I ran off to our rooms before the main course to admire our new presents. Grandmaman de Neuchâtel, referring to us, asked around the table: *"Mais qu'est-ce qu'ils deviennent, les poulets?"* ("Where are the little darlings?") *Poulet*, meaning chicken, is also used as a term of endearment. To which Grandmaman de Lausanne retorted: *"Ben, ils sont dans notre assiette et on va les manger!"* ("Well, they're on our plates and we're about to eat them!") My mother always contended that her mother was born at the wrong time. She would have liked to go to college, and with her keen intellect would have excelled in her studies. But being that she was born in 1887, when girls did not attend university, she had to settle for the traditional role of wife and mother. To satisfy her enormous curiosity, she devoured books. When she turned blind in her seventies, she relied on my mother and my aunt to read to her, engaging them in animated discussions.

Grandmaman de Lausanne met her future husband, my grandfather, when he became her algebra tutor. Her father, director of the newly created Telephone Company in Neuchâtel, insisted that his daughter work as a *téléphoniste*, an occupation she loathed (when no one was watching, she'd pull out a book and read—that's how she taught herself Italian). Her mother rented out a few rooms to boarders; Grandpapa was one of them. He was shorter than she was, always stood erect, a dashing, self-confident dynamo, teaching business at the Ecole de Commerce in Neuchâtel. His technique was straightforward. Whenever he caught a student nodding off, he would throw his set of keys on the errant student's desk, harshly bringing him back to reality. Test results (with 10 being the highest grade) were announced as follows:

"First: 10. Second: 9. Third: 8. Everyone else: 0!"

The rationale for this type of instruction? In business you have to be quick. My grandfather taught for several years, first in Neuchâtel, then in Lausanne, where he moved with his young wife. He didn't get along with his mother-in-law, who had told him shortly after their wedding, "My daughter will always remain my daughter." When World War II broke out, he joined the military, and quickly rose to the rank of *colonel divisionnaire*, which corresponds to a four-star general in the U.S. Army. (The Swiss Army doesn't have generals in peacetime; in times of war one general is selected from a pool of colonels.) Years later, while traveling through various parts of the country, Grandpapa was always recognized and remembered fondly by the men he had led—and even those he had instructed. As soon as the war ended, he left the army and became a businessman. No one knows exactly what he did besides sit on the board of numerous (seventeen at one point) companies. My mother told me that money was made, and lost in the crash of 1929, when Grandpapa invested funds he didn't have, thereby forcing the family to make sacrifices. (It was Grandmaman and the kids who were expected to tighten their belts; my grandfather, very attached to his 1928 Buick, refused to give it up.) Action was what Grandpapa loved above all else. He would buy shares at one Franc, turn around and sell them at two. According to Maman, if he had only kept them a while longer he could have become a millionaire. Evidently, he was more interested in the excitement of buying and selling stocks than in acquiring millions.

Grandpapa de Lausanne had suffered the loss of his mother at the age of seven. Until the day he died, he was reminded of her funeral whenever church bells rang. His father, considered a wealthy man (he owned several buildings in Couvet), subsequently married a woman my grandfather hated. Around 1900, at a time when there were only three cars in the entire canton of Neuchâtel, he and his father went to Paris to buy a car, most likely a De Dion Bouton. The model they bought had neither roof nor steering wheel, just a vertical bar with a lever to steer the vehicle. It took them five days to get back from Paris. Later, when Grandpapa was engaged to my grandmother, he took her for a drive in the country. She must have been duly impressed when he smashed into a barn and came to a halt in the middle of a room where the farmer and his family were having their Sunday lunch. Grandpapa's love affair with cars began on that trip to Paris. Over the years he owned several American models, and while he was in the army he got around in a black, chauffeur-driven Studebaker.

My grandparents had two other children besides my mother. The eldest, a boy born with a congenital hip dislocation which caused him to limp his entire life, did not live up to my grandfather's expectations and went on to become a mediocre lawyer. The middle child, a girl, had the misfortune of showing artistic talent and was made to study business instead. That left my mother, the youngest, and my grandfather's favorite. Maman was everything he had looked for in a son: smart, athletic, fearless. She was so eager to study medicine that she told him, "If you allow me to study medicine, I promise I won't get married." Things didn't quite work out that way: my mother not only studied medicine, but ended up marrying a doctor.

My father, on the other hand, was an only child doted upon by a mother who, in turn, did not show a great deal of affection for her husband. My grandmother was one of eight or nine children, daughter of a judge in Couvet who, coincidentally, rented an apartment in a building owned by my maternal great-grandfather. Grandpapa de Neuchâtel was the first one of my grandparents to die and my memories of him are faint. But I remember his uncanny ability to make things—miniature papier-mâché houses for my brother's Märklin electric train set, rocking chairs, and other pieces of furniture. Because my grandparents were modest people with modest ambitions (Grandpapa worked as a postal clerk in Neuchâtel), they were unprepared for their son's exceptional gifts. By his late teens, Papa had become an accomplished pianist who was also drawn to the field of medicine, which, in the end, prevailed. For the rest of his life he played the piano every day, unless he was ill. Sometimes, on trips, he would seek out a hotel's piano, enjoying it even if the instrument was out of tune. My paternal grandparents sacrificed a lot to give the best to their son—paying for him to go to university, to belong to the *Zofingiens*, a male student society, to take piano lessons with Monsieur Veuve. In order to make ends meet, they ate, for the most part, bread and sardines.

When both sets of grandparents congregated at Christmas, they were quite formal, addressing each other as Monsieur, Madame, never the familiar *tu*. I always sensed my mother tensing up prior to such gatherings. For me, those were occasions to sample the best possible food, and gobs of it, if you included all the chocolate and candy my maternal grandmother gave me. I still have, neatly folded between the pages of an old photo album, the original menu from 1957 that I must have typed, very carefully, on Maman's ancient Remington. It reads:

Le grand bouquet de crevettes roses.

Le poulet de Bresse à la Mascotte.

Le buisson de pommes paille.

La gourmandise de petits pois.

Les cœurs de salade Mère Yvonne.

Le choix de fromages Franco-Suisse.

La corbeille des Hespérides.

La bûche de Noël flanquée de mille douceurs.

Les vins choisis.

The lyricism of this menu doesn't translate well into English. In essence, the meal consisted of shrimp, chicken, French fries, peas, salad, cheese, fruit, cake and wine. With regard to the succinctness of the English language, it always amazes us Frenchies that in English you can sign off on a letter with one single word: Sincerely. In French, we might say: *"Je vous prie de bien vouloir agréer, chère Madame, l'expression de mes sentiments les plus distingués."* ("I ask you to please accept, dear Madam, the expression of my most distinguished feelings.") As an English-speaking adult these days, I am amused by the verbosity and grandiloquence of my first language. But growing up in a French-speaking family, I thought nothing of using such flowery language myself.

Besides good food, Christmas also connoted the beginning of *les vacances d'hiver*. On December 26th my mother, JC and I would drive up to the mountains for three weeks of skiing. My father always joined us later. Before the chalet was built in St. Luc, my parents rented apartments in various ski resorts: Zermatt, Verbier, Grindelwald. Like most Swiss children, JC and I learned to ski at a young age. My mother was our teacher, and my father took many movies of her swooshing down the slopes, kids in tow. When she began to ski in the 1930's, ski lifts didn't exist. Skiers affixed sealskins to the underside of their skis, which prevented them from sliding back; when they got to the top they removed the skins, wrapped them around their waists, and skied downhill. Up and down the hill they went, for as long as they had the energy. In those days, outfits were neither lightweight nor waterproof, and least of all aerodynamic. Women wore skirts, although Maman preferred her father's military clothes from WWI, made of heavy, itchy wool. By the time her children were born, ski lifts were commonplace. Nevertheless, she sometimes agreed to *faire l'assiette*—act as a ski lift herself—when I got tired and whiny. She'd stick one of her poles between my legs, and with the "plate" acting as support for my behind, she would pull me uphill.

After a full day on the slopes we were happy to return to the chalet and relax, while Maman prepared dinner: *croûtes au fromage* (fried slices of white bread with melted cheese on top, served with Dijon mustard), *croûtes aux champignons* (same idea but with mushroom-and-cream topping), homemade pizza, or perhaps cheese fondue—which my mother only made when my father wasn't with us because he didn't like it. Whenever we had fondue, my brother and I were allowed to dip sugar cubes into tiny glasses filled with Kirsch, the Swiss cherry brandy. Those Kirsch-soaked cubes, to be swallowed just before they disintegrated in our fingers, were delicious, and our early introduction to hard liquor. What Papa preferred was *raclette*, another cheese specialty from Switzerland. To make *raclette* you need a half wheel of cheese, which you place on an open fire until it starts to melt. You then scrape—*racler*—the melting cheese onto a plate garnished with *cornichons* (gherkins), cocktail onions, small boiled potatoes, and a serving of *viande séchée des Grisons* (thin slices of air-dried beef), consume, and repeat until sated.

During those years I hardly ever saw my mother relax. It was as if that were unacceptable in our family, even on holidays. She certainly never relaxed when my father was around. In perpetual motion, she cooked, cleaned, did the laundry, shopped for groceries, tended to her vegetable garden (this being a form of relaxation), endlessly washing, peeling, cutting up the fruits and vegetables she grew in the ploughed land below the chalet. Later in the evening, after all activity had ceased in the kitchen, she would retreat to her room and sew, making curtains or pillow covers, darning what needed to be darned, altering what no longer fitted. My father typically sat in the *salon,* a small room taken up completely by his beloved piano, a Bechstein grand that looked incongruous in the rustic chalet. Bringing it to the chalet had been quite a feat, though not as formidable as when my father purchased a six-and-a-half-foot long Steinway in the late sixties. That piano had to be hoisted up to our top-floor apartment in Berne with a crane—one of those large yellow ones used in construction. I came home from school with a girlfriend and stood in the courtyard with other curious onlookers, while the piano, its legs removed, was raised and tilted so as to fit through one of the windows. The whole operation took hours.

My father played the piano every night at the chalet, and since my minuscule room was right above the *salon,* I would fall asleep to the sounds of classical music.

Growing up I was interested in finding out more about how my parents fell in love. Maman would scoff, as if she deemed it a subject of little interest. It took me years to piece together the whole story—if that, in fact, is the whole story. According to her, the promise to her father was made in good faith. My grandfather, secretly pleased, let her matriculate at the University of Lausanne. In the 1930's in Switzerland, girls had to be nineteen to take their baccalaureate exam, while boys could take it at eighteen. My mother passed her *bachot* and began her medical studies. She and a handful of other females sat in the back of the lecture hall and kept a low profile. Six months later, suffering from stress-related angina, Maman took a leave of absence that would last one year. Doctor's orders: do not open any textbooks. So she didn't. She biked, she hiked, she skied, she played tennis. That summer, with her parents' blessing, she went off to Chiemsee, in Bavaria, for some R&R. There she met Lotte, a children's tutor for a well-to-do family, with whom she developed an enduring friendship.

Maman resumed her studies in 1937. Within six months she had succeeded in passing the first of three exams (*propédeutique* or *propé* for short). She continued to enjoy all her classes, even anatomy, where students had to dissect corpses crawling with maggots. Once, after a dissection, Maman took home, wrapped in a newspaper, the skeleton of the poor stiff's arm.

During the 1938 summer holidays, she spent several weeks babysitting for a family near Kaiserslautern. Later, she traveled to Munich to see Lotte, and met a cousin of hers, Hanko, at her parents' house. This fellow, a doctor, amateur pianist, cultured, intelligent, took an instant shine to my mother, but she was turned off by the way he, or rather his clothes, smelled. Nevertheless, they spent some time together, going to an Edwin Fisher concert, visiting Partenkirchen in the Bavarian Alps, even attending a Hitler rally. At the rally Hanko, an admirer of Hitler, and everyone else in the audience stood up and saluted. All except my mother, who remained seated, trying to make herself as inconspicuous as possible. The Hitler factor must have played a role in Maman's dislike of Hanko—that, and the fact that he had asked her to sew on one of his buttons on their first or second "date."

In July 1939, at the invitation of an English friend, my mother crossed the Channel and spent a month in Bognor Regis, on England's south coast. She got a job at a nearby boarding school, which she enjoyed very much. When war was declared in September, she didn't worry about the possibility of being stranded in Britain. Things appeared calm, she was having a good time, she just wanted to stay a bit longer. Her parents tried to convince her to come back right away, but she paid them no heed. It was only when she found out that the last convoy to the Continent was leaving in November that the seriousness of the situation dawned on her. Maman left England on that convoy. The trip took seventeen grueling hours, first by boat, then in a packed, darkened train (the blinds were pulled down to prevent passengers from knowing their whereabouts). At last she arrived in the small town of Vallorbe, on the French-Swiss border, where her father stood waiting on the platform.

In 1940, after she passed her second *propé,* my mother spent two months—one in surgery, the other in internal medicine—as an intern at Les Cadolles, a hospital in Neuchâtel. At the end of the first month, my father, himself an intern, took over her spot. Athletic and outgoing, Maman had already made a number of friends; when they needed an extra tennis player, she invited my father to play, an invitation he readily accepted. Eager to keep up with her, Papa took up skiing and biking. (After he won her heart, he gave up those sports because he didn't excel at either.) Maman, an avid cyclist, toured the country with three other students one summer during the war, when few cars were seen on the road. The other woman in the group stayed behind in the Grisons, and Maman finished the trip accompanied by her two male companions, one of whom was crazy in love with her. At night the three of them slept in a tent, my mother wedged in between the lads—nothing improper ever took place, she assured me. She also skied every chance she got. One brutal winter, she and a classmate stayed at an unheated chalet in the mountains that belonged to a friend of her father's; every morning they'd wake up with icicles on their duvets, formed by their freezing breath during the night. They had so little money that all they consumed was milk, figuring it would provide the necessary nutrients.

My mother's daily life during those wartime years was not affected much, except for the rationing of food. Uninterested in politics, she never read the papers, and remained engrossed in the bubble of her academic world. Although her parents loathed Hitler, war wasn't a topic of discussion at home.

Maman graduated from med school in 1943. My father had finished a year before and immediately accepted a position at the Inselspital in Berne. Once during their engagement my mother, who often had bouts of angina when she saw him, insisted they take a break from each other for six months. Already then she harbored doubts about the viability of such a union. But, as she told me throughout my adolescence, she was so taken with my father's intellect and his musical gifts that she ignored the little voice that said, "Maybe he's not the one." In April 1944, my parents tied the knot.

So much for my mother's pledge that she would choose medicine over marriage. In reality, the choice was made for her. Women in Switzerland in the 1940's could not have it all—they either chose a profession or chose to have children. My mother didn't really practice medicine until I left the house at eighteen. She briefly worked in audiometry in 1960 (as a reaction to something my father had said to her) and psychosomatic medicine, where she administered Rorschach tests to patients, but she didn't care for it. While my brother and I were growing up, she prepared herself for the day she would work in her anointed field. As the spouse of a university professor—which my father became in 1954—she could attend as many classes at the University of Berne as she wanted, free of charge. She took full advantage of that policy, auditing classes in medicine (except those taught by her husband, of course) and psychology to keep abreast of the latest developments. And prepared she was. In 1972, at the age of fifty-six, she was offered a part-time position in the newly created department of phoniatry at the Inselspital, the same hospital where my father worked. She happily practiced medicine for sixteen years, earning the respect and gratitude of both colleagues and patients. The only person whose respect she did not earn in the process was my father.

In October 1945 my mother, six months pregnant, started to feel contractions and gave birth to a premature baby. Claire died ten minutes after she was born. Maman chose not to hold her daughter, believing that she would be even more devastated if she laid eyes on her. Exactly a year and a day later, my brother was born. It was a difficult pregnancy. In the sixth month, it looked like Maman was going to give birth to another premature baby. By staying in bed for the rest of her pregnancy, she managed to bring a healthy boy into the world. Two weeks later she had a massive thrombosis of the pelvis and legs, and spent the next two months immobilized, not daring to lift up her head for fear of developing an embolism. A blood clot in the femoral artery of her left leg forced her to wear a special support stocking ever since then. Blood-thinning medication didn't exist at the time, so regular walks to increase her circulation were prescribed. Maman didn't mind, as she had always enjoyed hiking.

Hiking is Switzerland's national pastime. Hikers of all ages carrying backpacks can be espied throughout the country. They are simply part of the scenery. (Which doesn't mean that the Swiss don't love their cars: they do. Magnificent specimens of Italian, German and French design roar along impeccably maintained highways.) When I was small, like thousands of other Swiss children I *had* to partake in this patriotic activity. My favorite part of the hike involved food: stopping for a bar of chocolate, picnic lunches of *miettes de thon à la tomate* (canned tuna in tomato sauce) on a fresh baguette, or *cervelats* (sausages) grilled on the open fire and slathered with mustard. Running down the trail at the end of the day was nice too—it meant the hike was nearly over. Maman told endless stories to keep me from noticing that I was climbing far and wide. My first serious hike was to the Diavolezza in the Grisons, an all-day affair involving an altitude differential of 3,000 feet (yes, I could have used meters, but it sounds so much better in feet). I was four and a half, and Maman didn't stop recounting fairy tales until we were back at the chalet. As a child, she too was obliged to go on hikes. Only with her father the colonel in charge, it took on a slightly more regimented look. Grandpapa always wore a three-piece suit and hat, no matter what. Old photographs show him standing over his brood amid the mountain pastures, as if tending a flock of sheep: his wife in a long, flowing dress, his two daughters, also wearing dresses, and his son, in a suit with short pants.

I don't mind hiking, as long as it doesn't involve roughing it. Given a choice, I will always opt for the plush velvety carpet of a four-star hotel, rather than the bare cold floor of a mountain hut. The absolute worst hike of my life took place in the summer of 1959, while we were vacationing in Zermatt. Papa had the bright idea of wanting to climb the Breithorn (elev. 15,000 ft.) with my brother, who was then thirteen. All the mountain guides were booked that day, the first sunny day after much rain, so Papa decided he would act as our guide. He bought a rope and off we went, our goal the *cabane* of Testa Grigia on the Theodule Glacier (elev. 11,500 ft.), located at the foot of the Matterhorn, where we would spend the night. I remember the climb. I was only eight, but I remember that climb. Oh, at the beginning it was a fairly typical hike—the sun shone, my mother told stories, and we stopped regularly for snacks. But then dusk fell. We were hiking on a glacier, roped to each other, my father leading the way over cracks and crevasses with his pick, JC behind him, yours truly, my mother at the end. Although my father was an accomplished climber, he was not a professional guide. The climb took much longer than expected. I cried, begged my parents to turn back. Instead, we plodded on and arrived at the refuge around eight in the evening.

At last, we thought. But unfortunately, there was no room at the inn. The *cabane* was full, not a single bed available. The place was in total chaos, because so many people had decided to hike that day. Try the other *cabane*, my parents were told, but they weren't about to drag me on another hike with no guarantee of a bed there either. I can still see the hallway overcrowded with people lying on mattresses. Finally an Italian maid took pity on us. She gave us her own bed, a very narrow bunk bed from which my mother struggled not to fall, having placed me near the wall for safety. As for the men in the family, they ended up sleeping on the floor—in front of *les toilettes*. At dawn the following day, Papa and JC set on their climb. (Later my brother complained to my mother that Papa was too slow for him.) Meanwhile, Maman and I watched people ski on the sun-drenched glacier. As soon as the men returned, we made our way back to Zermatt. I wouldn't be surprised if I ran all the way down. I wanted to put as much distance between me and the Theodule Glacier as I could.

Some hikes were fun, though. I had a friend, Nancy, who spent summer vacations in Les Haudères, a village in the valley next to ours. On the appointed day, Nancy and her dad would climb up to Col du Torrent, while Maman and I climbed to the same pass from the Val d'Anniviers. At noon, all of us reunited, we'd picnic together, feasting on the sweeping view as well as the food. Afterwards, Nancy would climb down with us and stay in St. Luc for a few days, or I would go back with her, staying at her parents' chalet in the Val d'Hérens until my mother picked me up, by car, later in the week. I'm sure we were not the only families engaged in this type of child swap.

I don't remember our apartment in Liebefeld, the neighborhood in Berne where my parents settled when they returned from the States. But the first film my father took in 1953 tells all: I am two years old, sitting on a swing in the garden, and my brother is pushing me as he feeds me porridge every time I swing back. Occasionally he misses and I struggle to catch the spoonful in my open mouth while holding on to the straps. My brother smiles impishly; I look dead serious. Feeding time, already at that tender age, was no joking matter.

As I grew older I noticed that my father was always the one taking pictures. Maman explained that in the beginning she did take pictures of us, but because she was including other people besides our family, my father got annoyed and decided to control the camera's output. Papa took many reels of movies during my childhood, and I'm glad to be able to revisit those times with actual footage of our holidays, mostly in Italy.

We lived in Liebefeld until Papa was named Professor of Internal Medicine. This promotion meant that my parents could now afford a bigger place. Maman would have preferred a house with a garden, but Papa saw a spacious apartment facing the Gurten—Berne's very own mountain, albeit of modest proportions—and he was sold. That is the home of my youth. It took up the entire top floor of a nondescript building on Roschistrasse. An old-fashioned lift brought us to our own landing. The new residence included three bedrooms, a *salon* with marble fireplace, sunny dining room with a view of the Gurten and the tract of farmland in front, and what we called *le fumoir* (the smoking room), more casual than the *salon*. The bathroom had a second door leading directly into my parents' bedroom.

Off to the side, a small hallway where we hung up our coats led to another W.C. The apartment had four balconies—one of which, the kitchen's, was the scene of my near demise when the strap holding the heavy awning became tangled around my neck; by chance, a neighbor across the street saw what was happening and immediately called my mother, who came to the rescue and scolded me for fooling around with the strap in the first place. There was a long corridor where I once collided with Maman just as she emerged from the kitchen carrying a large pot of hot soup. Luckily, the burns on my chest left no permanent scars.

Life at the Roschi, as we called home, proceeded without major incident until the day I thought I was going to kindergarten. Maman had dressed me in a pretty coat. I entered the *salon* to say goodbye to my father, who was playing the piano.

"*Au revoir, papa.*"

"Goodbye, my darling." He kissed me while he continued to play. "Where are you going?"

"Kindergarten!"

The playing stopped. Papa's smile vanished and piercing blue eyes bore into me.

"Where?" He stood up and, speaking in a loud voice, demanded an explanation from my mother who had discreetly opened the front door, pressed the elevator button and stood ready to bolt with the elevator door open. I saw her close the elevator door and re-enter the apartment, while my father berated her for trying to sneak me into kindergarten. A few minutes later, the piano playing resumed. In my room, Maman took off my coat. I cried, not understanding why Papa was mad and why I wasn't going to kindergarten. Perhaps my mother cried too, although she was loath to do so, especially in front of her children, having been brought up to believe that crying was for sissies. To pacify me, she promised me ballet, eurhythmics and piano lessons.

The reason my father had reacted so vehemently, I found out later, was because he was dead set against sending his kids to a German-speaking school. Since the Ecole Française de Berne, where both my brother and I were to be schooled, didn't offer kindergarten, the only option was to have us attend a local school. My mother, keen on the idea of sending her children to kindergarten, had evidently gotten her way with JC. Now it was my father's turn to exercise *his* right to do as he wished. Case closed.

Some people think that "Swiss" is the official language of Switzerland. In reality, there is no such thing. Switzerland is home to four national languages: German, French, Italian and Romansch. The majority of the population speaks *Schwyzerdütsch* (Swiss German), a dialect of German. As *Romands*—members of the French-speaking community—residing in

German-speaking Berne, we were part of a linguistic minority. My father grew up in French-speaking Neuchâtel and took pride in his excellent diction. Sending his children to a school where they would have to speak Swiss German was anathema to him. He viewed *Schwyzerdütsch* as an uncouth language—and yet spoke it every day at work.

My mother kept her promise. She enrolled me in a ballet class taught by a flashy Russian *émigrée*, a Jaques-Dalcroze class where we shook tambourines, and found a piano teacher. Apparently, I was a natural on the piano. Soon my first teacher had to be replaced by a second, more challenging one. (Years later, that second teacher, Madame Bovet, told my parents she couldn't handle me any longer and recommended a male teacher.) I don't know how Maman was able to convince me not to say anything to Papa until Christmas, when I surprised the assembled family members by playing a little tune. From then on I always played at Christmas, as did my brother and father.

I entered first grade and loved it. The Ecole Française represented a small enclave of *Romands* in a sea of Swiss Germans. My friends were schoolmates or children of my father's colleagues. In connivance with my mother, I also acquired a few Swiss German friends, one of whom, Marlies, lived on our street. An older girl, Marlies was mysteriously brought up by her grandparents. Her mother was either dead or divorced (being dead was preferable to being divorced in Switzerland at that time); as for her father, he was never mentioned. It was all very intriguing, that and the way Marlies' grandmother always played the same Chopin Waltz (Op. 64, Nr. 1) on her slightly off-key baby grand. I kept mum about my Swiss German friends in my father's presence, and all was well.

I decided at nine or ten that it was time for me to wear proper ladies' stockings, not the silly socks that were customary for girls my age. My mother laughed when I suggested it. That made me even more determined. As soon as she left the *chambre conjugale* I rummaged around in her lingerie drawer and helped myself to some flesh-colored hose. Every morning I'd leave the apartment wearing girlie socks. On the ground floor of our building, I'd wait until the coast was clear, slip off the socks and put on Maman's delicate nylons, feeling all proud and grown-up. There was only one problem: I didn't know I needed a garter belt to hold them up. After a few steps, the stockings would slide down to my ankles, and when they did I must have looked even more ridiculous than if I had been wearing those girlie socks. The way to school, along Monbijoustrasse, followed the Number 9 tram route. While walking, I desperately tried to hold my thighs together to keep the stockings up for as long as I could. But after a few steps I had to stop again, and every phone booth on the way to school became a changing room. Never mind that the booths had glass panels and the world, particularly people sitting in the passing streetcar, could observe my shenanigans. I wasn't about to ask Maman why the stockings kept falling down, nor could I ask my friends, who'd surely take me for a fool.

I enjoyed ice skating at the city's KaWeDe rink. One year Maman entered me in a costume competition where I showed up as Little Red Riding Hood. The following year, the same outfit morphed into a fancier version that included blond tresses made from horsehair and two papier-mâché doves, one precariously attached to my wig, the other on my shoulder (I didn't win). My mother was extremely skilled with her hands, and often came up with original designs. On one occasion, she concocted two dolls from a coconut she sawed in half. She scooped out the flesh and, placing each dry, half-shell on top of a small can, painted an exotic face on the bearded coconut. Then she added colorful bits of material to fashion a tiny scarf, blouse and skirt, and voilà!—I had two extra dolls for my collection.

JC and I got along well—as well as siblings separated by gender and a five-year age gap can. I idealized my big brother, and secretly fancied every one of his good-looking friends. What I liked best was making fun of people together. We'd stand on my balcony and mock anyone who happened to land in our field of vision. All were fair game. We were kids, we had no shame.

In 1965, my father was invited by a German pharmaceutical company to go around the world promoting a new hypertension drug. The trip, first-class with all expenses paid, would last six weeks, and Maman, of course, would accompany him. I was sent to live with Papa's secretary, a hugely overweight, motherly woman who also happened to be a family friend. More importantly, she spoke French. I felt somewhat abandoned, and remember getting into minor arguments with Maman just before she left. Every weekday morning, my task was to bring an empty *bidon* (milk can) downstairs to our mailbox, to be filled later by the milkman. The day my parents were to leave I got mad at Maman and muttered something under my breath about *le bidon stupide*. Then, feeling guilty, I prayed that nothing would happen to them on their journey. Maman's postcards from far-flung locales—USA, Hawaii, Japan, Taiwan, Hong Kong, Cambodia, Thailand, India—made me envious, but as kids are notoriously adaptable I quickly became used to living with Madame Jeanneret, and even developed a sense of independence. After all, not many of my classmates had parents who traveled and left their children in other people's care. There were two exceptions, both of whom became my friends: Bella, from Ethiopia, had been sent to live with a Swiss couple, friends of my parents, by her ambassador father who wanted her to have a solid Swiss education; Wendy was a Californian whose parents decided to leave her with a Swiss family, also friends of my parents, while they toured Europe in their convertible. When Wendy landed in my classroom, not speaking a word of French yet smiling bravely, I took an instant liking to her and begged the teacher to let her sit next to me. During the course of the day I explained the school routine to her, in English, and we became fast friends. Bella, two years older than me, went to a girls' boarding school in Fribourg, but regularly came back to Berne where her adoptive parents lived. She had the most dazzling smile and got along with everyone. The two of us spent many holidays together, and her presence never seemed to annoy my father. In fact, he found her so charming that he invited her to come along with us to Venice one spring vacation.

A few months after my parents came back from their world trip, a new boy arrived at the Ecole Française. Coincidentally, he bore the same name as my father.

At sixteen, François, the oldest boy in the school, carried himself like a man of the world. He, his younger sister Jacqueline, their mother and stepfather had recently relocated from Egypt. Whether François' father was Egyptian or not I don't know, but François had definitely inherited someone's swarthy good looks—and it wasn't his mother, who had pale skin and blond hair and giggled a lot. This was not your typical Swiss family arrangement, and consequently, a source of endless fascination among the students. Unlike everyone else, I was not in the least bit interested in this boy who acted like a know-it-all, so confident of his effect on schoolgirls. The more they tried to get his attention, the more disgusted I became. And my disgust was sincere. I deliberately ignored him during our rounds in the park at mid-morning break, the highlight of which occurred when two designated students went to the bakery next door and came back with baskets full of *petits pains, croissants, brioches,* and positioned themselves at the park's entrance. The purpose of this ritual was to sell treats to the students, so they could snack while they walked for fifteen minutes. If I had the misfortune of running into François inside the school, I made it a point to show my irritation. This display of negativity began to arouse his curiosity. So much so that he made a bet with his friends that he could convince me to attend one of his parties. I must say, he worked hard to win his bet. Any attempts at speaking with me in school were fruitless—I simply refused to acknowledge his existence. His mere presence irked me. I found his smirk intolerable. Besides, I had designs on other boys, one in particular, who didn't even know I existed. Daniel was a handsome boy: tall with wavy black hair, and the clearest, most striking blue eyes. His father was a psychiatrist, and all of Daniel's siblings—there were five or six of them—had the same black hair/blue eyes combination. Well, Daniel didn't pay me any attention, but it didn't matter. Every morning on the way to school, I hoped to catch a glimpse of him at a busy intersection through which, if I was lucky, he would come flying down on his bike. Although he never looked at me, I liked to imagine that our eyes had locked for a split second while he whizzed by me, and I'd be on cloud nine for the rest of the day. (Years later I met Daniel at an art fair in Basel where I was manning a booth featuring avant-garde paintings. Not only had he become average-looking, but when he couldn't see the humor in the artwork around him I concluded that he had turned dull as well.)

François devised a master plan. He pumped my friends for information and discovered that I was going to Lausanne one afternoon to see my grandparents. He purchased a roundtrip ticket to Fribourg, the first station stop, about thirty minutes from Berne. After school he followed me to the train station and found his way to the car I had settled in.

"*Salut!*" he said, acting as if he were surprised.

"*Salut,*" I replied, too stunned to forgo my manners.

"Where are you going?"

"Lausanne," I mumbled, annoyed that my reading was being interrupted by him, of all people.

"Mind if I sit here?" Before I could answer, he plopped down on the seat opposite me and flashed a broad smile.

I felt most uncomfortable. Pretending to read a book can be quite tiresome: you have to remember to turn the pages once in a while, and I could feel François staring at my reflection in the window. Looking back, I realize he only had thirty minutes to execute his plan, so time was of the essence. He was silent for a few minutes, then asked:

"What book are you reading?" François didn't exactly have a reputation for being studious; on the contrary, rumor had it that his talents lay elsewhere.

It was useless to continue the pretense of reading, so I slammed my book shut and proceeded to admire the scenery. Now we were both engaged in a game of watching the other's reflection in the window. Softly, without his usual bravado, François said:

"I'm having a party this Saturday. Please come."

"I can't."

"All your friends will be there."

"I told you, I can't. My parents won't let me."

"Why not?" Somehow I didn't find his insistence unpleasant. In fact, my defenses were crumbling. For the first time, I took a good look at him. And what I saw made me melt. Inexplicably, I had gone from loathing this boy to wanting him to kiss me very, very badly.

"Okay, I'll ask them," I said.
We were arriving in Fribourg. François stood up.
"Seven o'clock on Saturday."
And he was gone.
I found out about the bet much later. By then it didn't matter: we were in love.

I never saw Maman lose her temper. Even when she used the carpet beater to whack her children, she didn't lose her cool. According to her version of events, she gave us both plenty of warning, which we chose to ignore. She would chase after us, but never managed to catch us. The carpet beater was her last resort.
"Bon, alors je vais chercher la tapette." ("Okay, then I'll fetch the carpet beater.")
I hated the way she'd go to the broom closet, take the *tapette* from its assigned hook, and walk me to my room (all of this without a word), where I had to bend over to take my punishment. I don't think the beatings were that painful, but the humiliation! Because she was the one who disciplined us—my father had made it very clear to his wife, early in their marriage, that she shouldn't bother him with issues involving the children; he didn't get married to have problems, he told her, he got married to have fun—the carpet beater was as good an option as any.
My brother and I were afraid of my father. Or rather, of his moods. We could tell, from the way he'd put his keys down on the chest of drawers in the hallway, whether or not he was in a good mood. We disappeared into our respective rooms, and Maman into the kitchen, the minute we heard the car drive up. The car door would slam, the elevator rattle, the front door open, and Papa would announce loudly: *"Bonjour!"* Or: *"Bonsoir!"*
That was our cue. We would emerge from our rooms to assess the situation. A smile was good news. A frown meant possible trouble. Papa had a natural authority about him which kept us on our toes. We didn't linger at the dining room table; as soon as the last morsel of food was swallowed my mother and I cleared the table. After the meal Papa would retreat to the *fumoir* for his post-prandial ritual: coffee, cookies, a cigarette (he stopped lighting up after his bout with tuberculosis, but let the cigarette dangle from his lips), a glance at medical journals while listening to the radio. We never owned a television because my father didn't want one. My greatest joy, therefore, was to visit people who had a set, like Gertrude—one in a long string of young women my mother hired to take care of us while she accompanied Papa on business trips—who was married and lived in a cozy little flat with a black-and-white TV prominently displayed in the *Stube* (parlor). In our home, entertainment consisted primarily of making

or listening to music—but only Papa's kind of music. I never dared play my two prized recordings, one of the Beatles and the other of the gospel singer Mahalia Jackson, while he was home. And I only listened to French *yé-yé* idols—Johnny Hallyday, Sylvie Vartan, Françoise Hardy, Adamo, Sheila, France Gall, Claude François—when I knew it was safe to do so. Other forms of entertainment included eating, the quality of the food evaluated during each meal. Again, we would take our cue from Papa's facial expression. First, a moment of silence while he tasted his food; then, the verdict.

A vigorous nod of the head and the awaited praise.

"*Fantastique, ce filet de porc, absolument fantastique!*"

Or else, the dreaded words.

"*Elle est beaucoup trop salée, ta soupe.*" ("Your soup is much too salty.")

My mother was on an extremely tight budget and became, out of sheer necessity, a performer of culinary miracles. With a monthly allowance of only 1,400 Swiss Francs to cover all household expenses, she managed to cook scrumptious meals. She also learned to cook in record time. That was due to the fact that she led a secret, parallel life. She'd leave in the morning shortly after my brother and I went to school and my father drove to the hospital. She rushed to the university to audit courses, did her supermarket shopping, rushed back home fifteen minutes before we showed up, looking like she'd been there all along, and then left again in the afternoon soon after the three of us had vacated the premises. (When I was growing up, it was customary for school children to go home at lunchtime, which, at my school, lasted from 11:35 am until 2 pm. Swiss moms typically cooked two full meals a day for their children and husbands.) When Maman asked my father for an increase in the household budget, he agreed on condition that she supply him with an itemized list of everything she bought. My mother balked at the idea and opted instead to make due with what she received—that way, at least, she didn't have to justify each purchase, whether it was a kilo of flour or a dress for a special occasion. The dress wouldn't be for her, but for me. My mother had devised a clever scheme whereby she brought exquisite silk patterns, acquired cheaply on her trips to the Far East, to a local seamstress (a Swiss German lady, no less), and while the seamstress sewed Maman's evening gowns and *tailleurs* (tailored suits), my mother cooked for both of them in the kitchen (those lunches had to be planned around my father's absences). This enabled Maman to acquire an elegant, one-of-a-kind wardrobe at minimal cost.

Maman had a general aversion to anything store-bought. She much preferred to cook and bake herself, rarely wore *prêt-à-porter* clothes, and enjoyed making toys for her children. She claimed to be the least artistic one in the family, but how many moms can build a miniature *guignol* (puppet theater) using wood strips, old towels, plus—the mainstay of every original thinker—scraps of fabric, and mount a show with homemade puppets shaped like owls? Much more credit should be given to people who can create gems from practically nothing, which is far more difficult to accomplish. My mother, to my mind, had that talent. With regards to her musical aptitude, we never had the opportunity to hear her play the piano, even though she took lessons as a child, because as soon as she heard my father play she stopped.

Another reason why Maman was so frugal had to do with the war. Although Switzerland remained neutral during World War II, food and gasoline were rationed and surviving on very little became a way of life. It is undoubtedly difficult for anyone who has had the good fortune not to experience the ravages and privations of war to comprehend what life must have been like in those lean years. Sadly, I did not inherit my mother's thrift, especially when it comes to paper products and scotch tape.

A family anecdote about the war goes something like this: My grandfather, *le colonel divisionnaire,* was sent by the commander-in-chief of the Swiss Army on a secret mission to France. His instructions were to make contact with two French generals—to what end remains unclear. In any case, since my grandfather had to travel incognito and he happened to resemble a well-known French politician, he decided to impersonate him on the train ride to France. Grandpapa wore civilian clothes and the brim of his cocked hat hid enough of his face to make the whole cloak-and-dagger undertaking successful.

Luckily, Hitler did not invade Switzerland. Opinion is divided as to why that might have been. Was it so the Nazis could maintain a secure place amid war-torn Europe in which to keep their loot? Or was it, as some would have it, because the Swiss Army built up such an incredible defense, using the Alps as a fortress, that the Germans gave up any notions of invasion? Huge hangars stocked with food, medicine and arms to last for several months, if not years, were indeed carved into the mountainside, and camouflaged airstrips, usable in an instant should the need arise, still dot the bucolic Swiss landscape.

Forsaking his illustrious grandfather's military values, my brother became a conscientious objector. As a result, he had to pay a fine and do *service complémentaire.* He tried, in vain, to get out of the mandatory *école de recrue* (basic training) by fooling the psychiatrist into believing he was mentally incompetent. As men who had willingly served in the military, both my father, a major in the Swiss Army, and his father-in-law found my brother's antics offensive.

Papa loved cars, and that passion I have inherited from him. For as long as I can remember I enjoyed playing with toy cars. On our long journeys to Italy, it was fun to guess the make and model of the cars we passed (for we were always passing cars; on the few occasions that my father allowed himself to be overtaken, it was by flashy sports cars—Ferraris, Maseratis, Lamborghinis). Having to compete with an older, well-informed brother resulted in my gaining much knowledge of car aesthetics, if not mechanics.

My parents started out as automobile owners quite modestly with a 4CV, a rather spiffy Renault that came out in 1947, followed by the Frégate, a larger model. After Papa was named professor, the cars grew more luxurious. I liked sitting in his Citroën ID and bouncing on the softest, deepest cushioned backseat one could ever imagine (of course, seat belts didn't exist back then). Both the Citroën ID and DS were cars with hydraulic power systems; when you got in, the car was pretty high off the ground, but as soon as you started the engine it would sink with a swish. At some point, we became a two-car family and from then on, my mother drove a bright red Morris Mini. Maman drove fast. She drove so fast she almost ran me over one day as I started to cross the street on my way back from school. Later on, when I asked her about it, she explained that she was running late and worried that she wouldn't make it home before my father. That was her greatest fear. Once, shortly before lunchtime, she ended up behind him at a red light. Panicking, she took a short cut. What saved her was the fact that our apartment building had two entrances and Papa always used the courtyard door, which was one level up from the street. Maman parked on the street side, ran into the building, and managed to get in the elevator seconds before my father arrived from the courtyard. By the time he reached the top floor, Maman was in the kitchen with her apron on (echoes of June Cleaver), dipping her husband's daily ration of pre-sliced, homemade French fries into the *friteuse*.

After a couple of Citroëns, my father's interest veered from French to English automobiles. He bought himself a Rover 2000, which was quite sporty. JC and I loved that car's powerful acceleration, its soft leather seats. My father, who owned two consecutive Jaguars, was hooked on British cars for several years. In his sixties, he changed gears again, driving a BMW.

Papa had impeccable taste in cars. In furnishings, it was debatable. Maman didn't particularly like those silk-covered Louis XVI *bergères*. She would have much preferred contemporary furniture, easy to maintain and comfortable to sit in. But Papa, having more disposable income and very definite ideas about decorating, bought antiques and filled every corner of the apartment with them. As a result we couldn't own a dog, which I longed for.

Thanks to Maman's enthusiasm for 20th century art, I was exposed from a young age to such luminaries as Picasso, Matisse, Cézanne, Van

Gogh, Toulouse-Lautrec, Chagall, Miró, Dali, Magritte, Modigliani, and homegrown Klee and Giacometti. We often went to exhibits together and I quickly developed a passion for abstract (especially Abstract Expressionist) painters: Mondrian, Kandinsky, de Kooning, Motherwell, Sonia Delaunay, Franz Kline, Morris Louis, Sam Francis, Hans Hofmann, Adolph Gottlieb. My mother, insisting that she was not an artist, spent hours interpreting the canvases we saw, discovering hidden meanings beneath each brushstroke. I loved Calder's primary colors, his witty designs and whimsical mobiles. Rothko and Pollock I detested: the latter because I felt his "dripped" paintings involved little effort, and were therefore unworthy of admiration, and the former because he painted the same thing over and over again, albeit in different colors. (Maman's explanation was that Rothko, who committed suicide, was painting his own coffin.) Among the French impressionists I liked Pissarro, Renoir, Degas. Gauguin, with his rich, warm color palette of exotic women, conjuring up a world so far removed from my Swiss roots, was a favorite. I also admired Seurat, the master pointillist, because I imagined it must have taken him a very long time to draw all those little dots (as in *Le Cirque*). Other inspiring artists included Rouault, a devout Catholic who drew numerous versions of Christ with such vivid colors and dramatic outlines that I didn't mind the religious connotations of his paintings; Henri "Le Douanier" Rousseau, of naïve painting fame; Raoul Dufy, a fauvist, for his atmospheric seascapes; Maurice Utrillo and his Montmartre scenes; cubists Georges Braque and Juan Gris, especially Gris' renderings of violins and guitars; Franz Marc, whose depictions of horses I found spectacular. While styles differed widely, a common thread seems to have been color. In sculpture I loved Henry Moore's oversize, semi-abstract pieces in stone and wood, Louise Nevelson's quirky, extravagant designs, Jean Arp's curvilinear shapes.

    I tried to emulate the look of an art gallery in my room by hanging several posters on the walls. The minimalist décor consisted of a free-standing, diagonally positioned bed, tall dried flowers arranged in copper pots on the parquet floor, and indirect lighting (achieved by twisting two lamp heads toward the ceiling). I spent many hours daydreaming there, fantasizing about becoming a painter, a pianist, a conductor, anything but a doctor.

    I was a headstrong child, so my mother has told me. When she forbade me to do something, I found a way around it, although my little schemes often backfired. I loved candy, and in that respect was no different from any other child. We always had cookies in the cupboard and Maman made desserts regularly, but there was no candy lying around the apartment except for those horrible mints Papa used to suck on. As a rule, children in those days did not receive allowances from their parents; therefore, I felt I had no choice but to steal money to buy sweets. I'd sneak into my parents' bedroom and open Maman's wallet. Her handbag usually lay on the dressing table, which made my task easier. Timing was crucial: I always made sure she was doing something at the other end of the long corridor before I went in. The best time to do it was when she was occupied in the kitchen, and I could hear her humming. I would quickly take a few Francs, never bills or the larger coins. All I wanted was to buy gum and candy at the kiosk near school. I looked forward to opening the Bazooka wrappers, with their tiny comic strips inside; the bright pink sugary gum tasted like heaven in my mouth. Or I might indulge in a Coca-Cola flavored frog, a Carambar, a pack of Sugus, a Cailler chocolate bar, a *bouchée au caramel*. My rationale for stealing from my mother was that she would never have given me money to buy sweets if I had asked.

Evidently, stealing ran in the family, although I didn't find out about my brother's shoplifting until much later. My mother got a call from a local merchant, who complained that JC and one of his friends had been stealing chocolate bars from his shop. If they returned the stolen goods the next day, he wouldn't call the police. When my mother confronted my brother, he confessed everything. The most puzzling part of the story is that the boys didn't eat the chocolate bars. They were left unopened, neatly stacked in my brother's room. So this wasn't about chocolate at all; it was about the thrill of stealing and not getting caught. Looking back, I'm glad my brother did *something* wrong when he was a kid.

As I reached puberty, JC was finishing his *gymnase* in the bilingual city of Bienne. He studied in the French section of the *gymnase*, but took his meals with a Swiss German family who was very fond of him. Maman and my brother, sharing a passion for literary discussions and philosophical debate, were close during those years. After he passed his *Maturité cantonale* at eighteen, JC spent six months immersed in piano—he had a Petrov in his room, an instrument I barely touched because I didn't like its muffled sound—before launching into his medical studies at the University of Berne. It was about that time that he stopped talking to my father. (I wasn't privy to their disagreement.)

Meanwhile, I desperately wanted to host a party for my friends. Maman had thrown birthday parties for me when I was a little, but never when my father was home. It seemed that only he could invite people; even Maman got in the habit of having friends over during her husband's absence. My parents hosted many formal cocktail and dinner parties, where I was expected to make an appearance in a pretty dress, eliciting compliments from the grown-ups. Since I knew I wouldn't be allowed to have a party, I began to imagine ways in which to plan one behind my parents' back.

Every time they went on an overnight trip, I would try to set one in motion. One day they told me they were going to Basel for the weekend, to visit a former patient of my father's. I promptly got organized. Several classmates were invited. I rustled up some drinks—mostly small bottles of Schweppes Tonic Water that were kept in the cellar. Things were going along nicely, except for one detail. I failed to anticipate that some parents might call mine up to confirm the time and place of the party. Daniel's parents did just that, shortly before my parents were supposed to leave. The jig was up. To my greatest embarrassment, I had to cancel the party. My punishment was to join my parents on the trip to Basel.

I never managed to have that party. But at least I was allowed to attend other kids' parties. Like François' party.

François' family lived in a large house in the Stadtbach neighborhood near the train station. The property had a slightly rundown air about it. The household consisted of François, Jacqueline, their mother, her husband, at least one maid, and a variety of friends and relatives passing through, on their way to or from some faraway location. The laissez-faire atmosphere with much partying, drinking, smoking (on the few occasions that I saw François' mother, she always had a cigarette in her hand), and little parental supervision had a magnetic hold on the classmates who were privileged enough to have become part of François and Jacqueline's inner circle. François' room on the top floor was pleasant, but the main draw was definitely the basement. It had stools around a bar in one corner, a record player with a wide selection of LP's, a couple of worn couches, easy chairs, throw pillows and scattered *poufs* (ottomans). In the middle of the room, a large Persian rug had been rolled to create a dance floor. The lighting was dim, conducive to deep discussions or gentle groping.

This is the house where, dressed in a simple skirt and blouse (I didn't want to give the impression that the party had any significance for me), I arrived shortly after seven o'clock one Saturday night. The front door was open; I stepped inside and stood, hesitating, in the rather sumptuous foyer. Where was the party? Feeling foolish, I considered leaving when François' mother dashed by, briefly introduced herself, and pointed to a door from which, at that instant, her son emerged. He looked like a movie star with his trademark scarf tucked inside his shirt collar. He grinned and led me down the stairs towards the music.

I knew all the people sitting around languidly, listening to records, dancing, talking, smooching. François carried on in proprietary fashion, as if I were his de facto girlfriend. He offered me a non-alcoholic drink, asked if I wanted to dance, looked into my eyes. I wasn't going to be swayed. I had come to his party to have a good time, not to be shown off as a trophy.

Around that time a few friends and I asked our parents for dance lessons. On Friday evenings a group of us took the tram to the dance hall, where we were taught basic steps in ballroom dancing. It was there that I met a tall, blond boy named André. André was nice enough (for a Swiss German, he spoke decent French), but his eagerness got on my nerves. I vividly recall him escorting me home after one of our lessons. As we said goodnight he clumsily leaned forward and applied his lips to mine. I didn't have any experience in that department, yet I knew this was not the way to kiss. I pushed him away, hard, because he kept on trying to kiss me. Finally, he let me go. I walked towards the apartment building; as soon as the door closed I spat into a handkerchief to wipe out all traces of André's transgression.

Having found out about the dance lessons, François decided to enroll too. In school he used every pretext to engage me in conversation. He pleaded with my friends to put in a good word for him. He was so determined that in the end, I gave in. After weeks of resistance, I allowed myself to be swept away by his good looks and apparent devotion. What did I know about love? I was a few months shy of fourteen, this was 1965, and we were living in Switzerland, a country where women still didn't have the right to vote on the federal level (that came six years later). His first kiss, his term of endearment for me *(petite fleur)*, the first time he cupped my breast during a dance lesson, his flair, his self-confidence: all of it made it impossible for me not to fall in love with him. My parents didn't suspect anything. François' name had come up in casual conversation, but never conjured up danger in their minds. My mother even let him spend a night at the chalet while he and two of his friends toured the region on their mopeds. My father wouldn't be there. Neither would my brother.

Now that I was a teenager JC showed more interest in my whereabouts. He would turn up unexpectedly on his bike when I was out with my friends, as if he were policing my activities. Did he deem my father to be remiss in his parental duties and decide to take on that role? Was it the role of a protector or that of a spy? It's true that Papa didn't get involved in the day-to-day affairs of his children; that was Maman's realm. Did she delegate some of those responsibilities to my brother or did JC take it upon himself to save me from falling in with a "bad" crowd? One evening in St. Luc my friend Mireille and I went to a café in the village, a fifteen-minute walk from the chalet. We sat at the bar and ordered lemonade when a boy I had a crush on walked in. His parents, from an old aristocratic family in Geneva, owned a splendid chalet not far from ours, and I always thought he was out of my league. Even up in the mountains these people, unlike the rest of us, looked refined. Christian saw me and sat on the stool next to mine, starting a lively conversation punctuated by much laughter. The barman, who knew everyone, joined in the fun while filling orders for other customers. The door opened and there stood my brother. He came straight towards me; I barely had time to say hello when he slapped me.

"You're coming home right now," he said, and marched out. I was too shocked to say anything. The pain of being humiliated in front of a boy I fancied was much worse than the slap itself. Mortified, I said goodnight to Christian. Mireille and I followed my brother at a safe distance. As soon as we arrived at the chalet, my mother berated me for going to the village in the evening without telling her. The rest of the holiday was ruined.

That fall, during school break, François and his friends stayed overnight at the chalet, camping out in their sleeping bags in the rec room downstairs. After dinner, François and I went outside and stood under the balcony. We kissed. He slid a deft hand under my thick sweater. One floor up my name was being called. That was the moment Maman chose to bring me out of a state of rapture. I didn't respond. We heard footsteps going back into the house and then, suddenly, she was downstairs, calling again. I quickly rearranged my clothes.

"I'm here," I said weakly.

Maman looked terribly cross. She ordered me to my room and told François, in no uncertain terms, that he and his friends were no longer welcome; they were to leave first thing in the morning. Angry, François mouthed off behind her back. I cried that night, fearing that François would no longer love me, hating my mother for making a mess of things. Now she was going to tell my father. And I would be punished, one way or the other.

François and his buddies left at the crack of dawn, but not before they had smeared the walls of the guest bathroom with their own feces. Maman remembers the parting gesture well. I, on the other hand, conveniently blocked the incident from my memory.

That fall vacation signaled a change in my relationship with François. Not long afterwards, the father of one of my classmates, a Protestant minister, informed my parents that at François' parties *some* kids were doing unspeakable things. (To this day, I maintain that the good minister had it in for François' entire family because his son had fallen in love with Jacqueline.) At home, suspicion set in; new rules went into effect. I was forbidden to attend parties at François' house. It made us want to be together even more. We became, officially, a couple, and as the girlfriend of the most popular boy in school, I gained status and grew bold. Lies, cover-ups, secret correspondence—every subterfuge kindled our passion.

Years later, when I complained to my parents about the way in which they conspired to send me to an all-girl boarding school in another city, they always gave the same answer: we did what was best for you, your grades at the Ecole Française were poor. But a more likely reason for my banishment to Lausanne (when most of my classmates were going to the *gymnase* in Neuchâtel) was my parents' fear that I would end up pregnant if I wasn't immediately removed from my group of friends. I knew, of course, nothing about contraception. Maman had been forewarned by Papa not to say anything to us kids about the birds and the bees. So I was winging it, and admittedly, playing with fire.

My parents were completely in sync about their decision to ship me off to boarding school. At one point I tried to talk to them, telling them I hadn't done anything wrong, insisting the rumors were false. But it was too late. Against a minister's insinuations, I stood no chance.

Off to Mont-Olivet I went in April 1967.

It was a sunny, fairly warm day. Grandpapa de Lausanne, who lived not far from the school, offered to bring me there. My parents, perhaps relieved to leave the task to someone else, acquiesced. I wore long pigtails, a pink and grey corduroy dress, white socks (the hateful socks again), and maryjanes that I had dyed pink for the occasion. Sitting across from Mother Superior in the formal reception room, I felt like I was about to enter a convent. My only exposure to Catholicism had been during our Italian holidays. Out of boredom while visiting churches, I sometimes crossed myself with holy water in an attempt to impersonate a Catholic. And now I was supposed to live with those strange, asexual beings who wore habits that barely showed their faces and a silver ring on their right hand to signify marriage to Jesus! This, it turns out, was my first relocation; and even though it didn't entail moving to another country, I experienced culture shock.

After Grandpapa was done charming Mother Superior, she called one of the nuns—they belonged to the Order of the Visitation of Mary—the bespectacled, stern-looking Sister Louise, who showed me to my room. I had requested a roommate, hoping that it would help alleviate my sense of loneliness, but as Sister Louise explained, I was fortunate enough to have been assigned a room of my own on the third floor, with views of Lake Geneva and the Alps in the distance. I looked at the dismal space I would occupy for the next three years and wanted to weep. As I unpacked my two red suitcases, a gift from Maman, a loud boom echoed through the long corridor. That was how meals were announced: a student, or a nun, would strike the majestic gong hanging above the stairs. A girl with wavy blond hair, Angelika, walked into my room and, without smiling, suggested I follow her to the dining hall on the first floor.

Angelika and I became friends. She admitted later that she was grumpy that day because she didn't want to show the new girl around, especially not one who looked so stupid with her pigtails and those horrible pink shoes, but a nun had instructed her to do so. Angelika's mother lived in Germany; her father worked in Zambia. Her younger brother was also at boarding school in Lausanne. Angelika was an old-timer, meaning she had been at the *pensionnat* for several years and only went home on major holidays. At least I could go home every weekend.

Up close, the nuns looked odd to me. Their outfits, black robes with a black veil held in place by a tight white bandeau, hid every strand of hair. A white wimple covered the neck, from which hung a solid silver cross. The Sisters all wore a chaplet on their belt. Those who did the cooking and the cleaning wore white habits and veils, and seemed to be treated with some disdain by their more educated counterparts.

It wasn't long before Angelika and I, along with five other classmates, started to rebel. The first revolt took place in the chapel where boarders were supposed to go for prayer every morning. All of a sudden, pretending to know the rituals of Catholicism was no longer appealing. We began to make noise in the back pews: sneezing, coughing, giggling. We fidgeted, we pushed one another. Then the Catholics in our clique stopped saying prayers altogether (non-Catholics, while forced to attend, were not expected to participate). We caused so much disruption that the nuns changed the rule: from then on, daily chapel attendance would be mandatory for Catholic boarders only—which made them furious, as they had hoped to be dispensed as well.

The second item on our agenda had to do with the uniforms we were required to wear. We decided our pleated, navy blue skirts were much too long, so we rolled up the waistband to achieve a more fashionable, well-above-the-knees look. Those of us (that didn't include me) who were generously endowed showed off a little cleavage to spruce up those starched white shirts and dull blue, or grey, sweaters. Many girls used make-up and colored their hair. I dyed mine jet black in the small sink in my room, applied red lipstick, and darkened my eyebrows with a black eye pencil. One day our English teacher, Sister Rita, came to my room right after I had finished coloring my hair. She looked at me, saw the messy sink, and shook her head. With a sad smile she said that God had made me the way I was, and why did I want to go and change what God had created?

Besides Angelika and me, the core rebel group included Carole, a lanky Swiss who had spent her childhood in Djibouti; Anne-Marie, coquettish daughter of the Swiss Consul in Morocco; Beatrice, a zaftig, defiant Swiss German from Zurich who didn't do well in her studies and couldn't have cared less; Françoise, a smart day student from a noble Vaud family; and Manou, another day student from Lausanne, small, vivacious, always dressed to the nines. In our class of twelve, we formed the majority. There were girls from other grades, hangers-on, who admired us and tried to follow our lead, but more timidly. And then there were those we swapped clothes with—that is, when we got out of our uniforms, on weekends and Wednesday afternoons. The girl with the most exquisite wardrobe was Georgina, a skinny English redhead who was best friends with one of Chaplin's daughters. Charlie Chaplin, a resident of nearby Corsier-sur-Vevey, sent his girls—all bearing an uncanny resemblance to their mother, Oona O'Neill—to Mont-Olivet. On Saturday mornings, when school let out at 11:30, a chauffeur picked them up in a large black car while the rest of us headed for the train station in a shared taxi.

The boarding school housed girls from all parts of the world. Some had parents who lived apart; others came from countries in political turmoil (Lebanon, Nicaragua) or with limited educational opportunities; yet others were there because Mont-Olivet had a reputation for being a serious, academically rigorous institution, unlike many of the *pensionnats* dotting Lake Geneva that functioned more as finishing schools. A few were dumped there because their parents, for whatever reason, couldn't deal with them—those were often girls who had access to the most pocket money.

I knew why I was there: to prepare for the *Maturité fédérale*, the Swiss university entrance exam. But also to be kept away from boys. Ah, boys! The nuns kept us safe from boys alright. The school, in a park-like setting, was situated in Montchoisi, not far from the Quai d'Ouchy. The property sloped towards the lake and was enclosed on all sides by a tall, wrought-iron fence. At the bottom of the property, that fence became a concrete wall. On the other side of that impregnable wall stood a boys' boarding school, Champittet, run by the *chanoines* (friars) of Grand-Saint-Bernard. On very rare occasions girls were allowed to glimpse that other species—boys—when joint dances were organized by the schools. I didn't attend any, since I went home every Saturday morning and returned on Sunday evening. Many kids from other *pensionnats* did the same: the train from Lausanne to Berne was usually full of boisterous boarders on the ninety-minute ride home. Sunday nights were a bit gloomier as we faced the prospect of returning to our respective prisons for another week.

My classmates and I were so deprived of masculine presence that we all developed crushes on the handful of lay, male teachers the school employed. One in particular, a history teacher, was the object of my desire. He was by no means dashing—not with his balding head, tiny mouth, birdlike features—and married to boot, but he was tall, self-confident, and, to my mind, sexy. He was in the habit of looking at our budding chests while speaking to us girls. That mere glance brought me to my knees. I took every opportunity to ask him questions, before and after class, or better yet, to "accidentally" bump into him in the hallway between classes—just to have him stare at my breasts. Sometimes he lightly touched my elbow or shoulder, and I fantasized that he would leave his wife and we would embark on a passionate affair culminating in a fairytale wedding. Unable to concentrate during his daily lectures, I found history to be a total wash.

Even the nuns behaved giddily when a priest showed up.

It isn't surprising, then, that some of us acted out our frustration in strange ways.

When my parents sent me off to Lausanne, they assumed that François and I would no longer be able to see each other. Maman made it a point to pick me up at the *Hauptbahnhof* (main train station) on Saturday afternoon, then she would drop me off at the *Konservatorium*, in the heart of the Old City, where I had my weekly piano lesson with Herr Matter. Afterwards, she would be waiting outside in her Mini and we drove home—but not before stopping at a bakery along the way.

What Papa and Maman didn't know is that every Sunday night François boarded the same train, so that we could neck during the half-hour ride to Fribourg. When either parent accompanied me to the platform, François knew to hide and get on at the other end. And every Saturday, faithfully, he waited for me in one of the dark corridors of the cavernous Conservatory. I'd run into his arms and steal a few kisses before sprinting upstairs to get to my lesson. If I arrived a few minutes late, Herr Matter would warn me to be punctual next time, but with a twinkle in his eyes. (I think he had a soft spot for me, and definitely enjoyed the sight of my mini-skirts, which I kept pulling down while seated, until he finally exclaimed, "Look, if you're going to wear a mini-skirt, just wear it and stop fiddling with it!")

François and I continued our secret romance for several months. And then, inexplicably, I grew tired of the whole thing. He came to visit me in Lausanne a few times on Wednesday afternoon, when Swiss schools traditionally closed, and we would walk around, making sure no one from the school saw us. But soon I lost interest. One day I simply told him I didn't want to be his girlfriend anymore. He asked if I had found another boy. No, I hadn't found another boy. Where, pray tell, would I find a boy at an all-girl Catholic boarding school?

In February 1968, my parents allowed me to spend a weekend in London with a chaperone, the daughter of friends of theirs who lived in Lausanne. Catherine, four years older than me, was actively involved in the Moral Rearmament movement, whose headquarters were in Caux, above Montreux. I didn't know anything about Moral Rearmament, but I knew I wanted to go to London. Papa agreed to let me go only after Catherine assured him that she would take full responsibility for me. The nuns gave their assent because the purpose of the trip, a Moral Rearmament conference, seemed lofty enough; they were, perhaps, hoping for a conversion. The weekend's highlights included a speech by Rajmohan Gandhi, a grandson of Mahatma; a play, *Happy Deathday*, by Peter Howard; and a delicious meal at the Swiss Centre. Rajmohan fit all my fantasies of the darkly handsome, intelligent prince. When Catherine introduced me, my already weak handshake—a character flaw that irked Maman, an advocate of firm handshakes, no end—turned even limper.

I returned to Mont-Olivet with delusions of a religious awakening. That lasted for about a month. Then creative juices began to flow. In my small room on the third floor I spent hours choreographing Gershwin's Rhapsody in Blue, with a notation entirely of my own. I became briefly enamored of a boy I'd met on our weekly train runs. He wrote romantic letters, sent plush animals to the *pensionnat*, and generally made me feel loved and wanted. But he was quite small, and I didn't think of him as especially bright.

Competing for exoticism among Mont-Olivet's cosmopolitan girls, I came up with a fictitious family history that featured a Greek grandmother (by process of elimination, she had to be my paternal grandmother since I already had a Swiss grandmother on Avenue de Rumine), conveniently widowed and living the life in her plush villa in Athens. It seemed so boring to be Swiss, with Swiss parents who lived in Switzerland! My imagination thus unleashed, I turned my attention to two boys I saw every weekend at the train station, both of them sons of diplomats: one, of the Swiss ambassador to India; the other, the one I really liked, of the Ecuadorian ambassador in Berne.

Researching feverishly in the school library I wrote a lengthy essay on Ecuador, giving the impression that I had visited the country. I bought special vellum paper, wrapped a velvet ribbon around the oversize envelope and presented it with a flourish to the boy on the platform one Saturday, just before the train arrived. I waited for weeks to get a sign, a note, anything. For the rest of the school year, the Ecuadorian avoided me like the pest.

My American friend Wendy had an older brother, Perry, with whom, at her urging, I had started a pen-pal relationship. We wrote to each other irregularly, but when we did the letters were long, packed with drawings, poems, photos, assorted artifacts from our respective countries: a feather found on a Californian beach, a dried and pressed *gentiane* from the Alps. Topics ranged from the mundane to the sublime: the music we listened to, the drudgery of school, our dreams and aspirations, the pros and cons of using drugs (he smoked marijuana, I was against it), the Vietnam War, the meaning of love. When we began our correspondence Perry was still in high school in Palo Alto; he then went on to Berkeley. For me, Perry's letters represented an exciting slice of American life, filled with glamour, freedom, open-mindedness.

In June that year Bobby Kennedy was assassinated. Despite my lack of interest in politics, I remember the cloud that fell over the school during those somber days. Students talked about the Kennedy "curse," violence in America, the state of the world. But soon, as our young minds could not grasp the true depth of this tragedy, we settled back into our daily routine.

Wednesday afternoons were spent at my grandparents' where I entertained them with tales from the trenches while gobbling down pastries. Saturday mornings, right after biology—our teacher admonished us every week not to cross our legs, because that would break the capillaries, and we didn't want to develop varicose veins later in life, now did we?—I rushed to the train station in a cab, dressed much too elegantly for a sixteen-year-old. I even wore white gloves on occasion. Maybe my parents felt guilty for packing me off to boarding school. In any case, it was fun trying on outfits in Berne's fashionable boutiques while Maman sat patiently, waiting for me to choose something that would make me look older and appear sophisticated. Rubbing elbows with students from worldly families had had an impact on me. The pigtailed girl with the dyed pink maryjanes was no more.

Most afternoons after class, I practiced my piano in one of the music rooms located on the upper floor of the school wing. All buildings were connected by a maze of corridors enabling us to walk from one to the other without having to go outside. Although the pianos were old, I enjoyed playing my loud, modern pieces on them, while the rest of the girls stuck to scales, conventional *études,* or worse yet, Bach fugues. I didn't like the classics—Mozart, Beethoven—and was lucky to have a teacher who not only indulged, but applauded my eclectic taste. When I chose to play Gershwin's Preludes for a recital, Papa was shocked. Gershwin, in his view, didn't belong to the realm of purely classical music. Ravel, Rachmaninoff, Bartók, Chopin, Mussorgsky, Darius Milhaud, César Franck, Manuel de Falla—I loved them all. Partial to chords and syncopated rhythms, I shied away from dainty, predictable melodies that didn't allow for cheating. (What was the point of playing an instrument if you couldn't improvise, or better yet, *improve* on the original once in a while?)

Food at the boarding school was a far cry from the meals Maman cooked at home, but we all had our favorites on certain days of the week. Mine was a dish consisting of *chippolata* (miniature veal sausages) cut up in tomato sauce and mixed with rice. And for dessert, a Tam-Tam (yogurt-size container of caramel pudding). One Tam-Tam was never enough though, so we traded across the table, bartering an extra roll for another dessert under the weary eyes of the rather plump sister assigned to our table, who had long given up any attempts at disciplining her charges.

Snacks were not permitted in the boarders' rooms, but we all ignored that rule and stocked up on chocolate bars, cookies and sweets. I also kept a supply of Gala triple cream cheese on hand, delicious when spread on DarVida crackers.

Sometimes Angelika spent the weekend with me in Berne. Those were fun times—for her it meant freedom for a day and a half; for me, entertainment and companionship. Having lost touch with all my classmates from the Ecole Française, I was forced to form new relationships and Angelika was the first girl I had befriended at Mont-Olivet. She didn't talk much about her parents, yet I gathered that all was not well on the marital front. Her mother, a pretty brunette, lived in a small apartment in Karlsruhe; there were hints of a boyfriend or two. Angelika's father, tall, blond, rugged, worked as an engineer in Zambia and stopped in Lausanne whenever he came back to Europe on business. Angelika's brother, as handsome as his dad, was off limits.

In our last year at Mont-Olivet, a select few seniors were granted permission to move to the top floor, a great privilege according to the nun who oversaw us. The attic floor did feel exclusive. For one, it couldn't be reached by elevator, but only via a flight of stairs; it also had fewer rooms, and the view of the Alps was even grander. More importantly, it was much quieter, and we were going to need a lot of peace and quiet while preparing for our exams.

The exams in question, *la Maturité fédérale,* consisted of two parts: oral exams to be held in another city (in this case, Neuchâtel) six months before the written finals, which were to be taken in Fribourg. I was annoyed at my parents for sending me to a school that offered only the *Matu* (as we called it) *fédérale,* notoriously more difficult than the *Matu cantonale* (the corresponding state examination). The *Matu fédérale,* unlike the *Matu cantonale,* did not take into account school grades from the previous three years; in addition, candidates had to travel to other towns and be subjected to examination by unknown professors in daunting university halls. Had I gone to the *gymnase* in Berne like my mother wanted me to (after she saw how unhappy I was at Mont-Olivet and I begged her to get me out), I would have studied for the *Matu cantonale* and felt less pressure.

So study we did. But despite our rigorous pre-exam regimen, or perhaps because of it, I still managed to make a fool of myself. Naturally, it had to do with a boy.

Shortly before I was to take my orals, I met up with Perry. He had written that he was coming to Europe for a few weeks and wanted to see me in Lausanne. Filled with anticipation, I began to plan every detail of his visit. It would have to take place on a Wednesday afternoon, when we didn't have school. In the register by the front door where all boarding students had to sign in and out, I would put down my grandparents' address, as I usually did. I would take him to the Voile d'Or, a pricey restaurant located next to the marina in Vidy.

On the appointed day I arrived at the train station, where we had agreed to meet, with plenty of time to spare. I imagined Perry in stylish clothes, and stood by the main entrance waiting for such a figure to come out. I wore a white dress with large blue flowers, accessorized by a navy Chanel purse (I'm pretty sure it was an imitation, for I sincerely doubt Maman would have bought me an original), matching high heels, and dark glasses. Glancing at the large clock that showed every second pass with inexorable precision, I became nervous. We only had a few hours to spend together and Perry was late already. I hated to be late, and especially hated for other people to be late. From the corner of my eye, I noticed a man on a scooter who also appeared to be waiting for someone, but dismissed him as a motorcyclist of little interest. I was impatient to meet Perry, and getting angry with him for making me wait. Finally, at 12:25 (we had agreed to meet at noon), I admitted defeat: I had been stood up. Yet I couldn't bring myself to leave. The guy on the scooter had taken off his helmet. Something in his pose struck me as familiar. I stared. He stared right back. That can't be him, I thought, Perry wouldn't look like this, all disheveled, carrying a knapsack and riding a Vespa.

The man approached me tentatively.

"Monique?"

"Are you Perry?" I asked, my heart fluttering.

We shook hands.

"What are you going to do with that?" I pointed at the scooter.

"What do you mean?"

I giggled.

"You can't take it to the restaurant." He seemed confused. "We're taking a taxi."

I was back in control. Perry looked around for a place to park his motorcycle. Struggling in French, he asked a passerby where he could leave it. I quickly took over, showed him what to do. He secured the Vespa, taking his backpack with him. I was hoping he would leave the unsightly bag in one of the station lockers, but when I suggested it he said, with a wink, that it contained all his valuables. I stepped into the first cab waiting in front of the *gare* and Perry joined me in the back.

I felt an overwhelming sense of disappointment. Perry wasn't as handsome as I had expected him to be. He didn't behave with the confidence that exuded from his letters. And the scooter was a definite turn-off. Did he really expect me to sit on that thing in my pretty white dress?

In the cab Perry looked dazed, as if he were trying to figure me out, while I talked non-stop to mask my own state of confusion. On the one hand, I was thrilled to meet him at last; on the other, I was irritated by the clumsy, unromantic manner in which we had met. I wished we could go back in time and start all over again.

Lausanne is not a big town. In a few minutes we were at the Voile d'Or. I paid the taxi driver and led Perry through the restaurant's imposing doors. The maître d' offered us a corner table with a view of the lake. After Perry and I sat down, he excused himself and went to the men's room. I glanced around. Very few tables were occupied. The décor—linen tablecloths, silver cutlery, fresh flowers—lent itself to a perfect lunch, as did the subdued atmosphere.

When Perry returned, he seemed uncomfortable.

"This looks like an expensive restaurant," he began. "I don't have that much money . . . ."

"I'm paying," I said, annoyed at him for spoiling the moment with petty pecuniary concerns. "Please let's not talk about it." I opened my leather-bound menu.

"What would you like?"

After we ordered food—I went so far as to suggest wine to Perry, which he declined—we started to talk in earnest. By the end of the meal, we were both relaxed and had recaptured the exuberance of our letter-writing relationship. Perry explained that he had rented the Vespa to tour Europe (it was cheaper than renting a car and gave him more flexibility than the train). He needed to be in Berne, where he would stay with the same people who had taken in his sister a few years before, that evening. As we chatted I became more and more attracted to him and began to crave a kiss. We took a cab back to the center of Lausanne. I showed him the Gothic cathedral, the fifteenth-century Château Saint-Maire, the university. As we descended steps leading into a small park, he stopped and smiled at me, complimenting me on the way I looked. I took that as a sign and kissed him on the lips. He returned my kiss, with poise.

"Let's go to a hotel," I said.

I was seventeen years old, uninformed in the ways of contraception, and asking a nineteen-year-old man (he looked all man to me now) to accompany me to a hotel, only minutes from the *pensionnat* where the good Sisters were awaiting my imminent return from what they assumed was a weekly visit to my grandparents.

Perry didn't reply.

"Come on, let's go."

"Look, I'm really flattered, but I don't think it's a good idea."

"What do you mean? Aren't you attracted to me? You just said . . . ."

"You're a beautiful girl, but going to a hotel is not a good idea. It would spoil what we have."

Pouting, I started to climb down the steps. He continued to tell me why it was such a bad idea, but I didn't want to hear. I didn't hear the voice of reason, I heard the voice of rejection. All my expectations, hopes, romantic dreams dashed by a resounding *No*. Perry ran after me, held me by the shoulders, and kissed me once more, chastely. What a mess we had made of things. And now it was time for him to leave. He was off to Berne and I was going back to boarding school. Without spelling it out, Perry had made the cruelest of observations: I was still a kid.

We walked down to the train station and parted company in front of the big clock. It was almost five. I managed a weak smile. Perhaps, deep down, I knew that Perry—my Knight in Shining Armor, all the way from America—had saved me from myself.

Still a virgin, I went to Neuchâtel and took my orals. None of my classmates traveled with me as we were scheduled to be tested on different days. It was intimidating to arrive at the University of Neuchâtel, not knowing a soul, walking around those gloomy corridors in search of the proper testing room, a different one for each subject. On a podium behind long tables sat the examiners, pen in hand and stacks of papers in front of them, waiting for their next victim. Finding out later that I had earned a B in chemistry, a subject for which I had no affinity, reinforced my belief that such exams are absurd because they don't reflect the student's true knowledge. Six months later, we all traipsed off to the University of Fribourg to take our written exams, which would stretch over three days. In Latin, my best subject, I got a D because I developed stomach cramps just before entering the examination room.

The best part of the finals was coming home afterwards, getting into bed, and watching Maman wheel into my room a nicely laid out feast for two (Papa had a dinner engagement): smoked trout with lemon wedges, thin slices of white toast, a pot of hot tea, and an assortment of pastries. We ate while I recounted the day's events. When the phone rang, Maman rushed to her bedroom to answer it. I heard her say *"Merci, monsieur,"* and *"Au revoir,"* and then she was standing at my door, her face impassive.

"So? What did he say?"

A brief silence.

"You've passed!"

I jumped out of bed and screamed. Maman, laughing, congratulated me.

A while later, Papa came home. I ran up to him.

"Papa, guess what, I passed! I passed my exams!"

My father's answer stopped me dead in my tracks.

"Of course you passed, *chérie*, you're my daughter." He smiled, patted me on the head, and made his way towards the *fumoir*, mail in hand. I slowly walked back to my room. Maman put her arms around me before going to attend to her husband's needs.

My three years at Mont-Olivet had ended. The core group (Beatrice was the only one who flunked) promised to keep in touch. Angelika moved to Germany, and I went to have my wisdom teeth taken out. After the procedure, I lay low for a week. Then I made an appointment to talk to my piano teacher about becoming a pianist. Herr Matter and I met in a little café under the arcades in the *Altstadt* one spring afternoon. After we exchanged pleasantries, he asked if I would be willing to practice the piano eight hours a day, every single day.

I made a face.

"If you're not sure, I recommend that you spend a semester at the Mozarteum in Salzburg. But I have to warn you, it's going to be hard work. And you'll have to play Bach, Mozart, Beethoven, whatever they say."

Herr Matter knew how much I loved non-traditional works. We kept on chatting. I mentioned that I had recently attended a concert led by a female conductor and had been entranced by the notion of a woman conducting an orchestra. Herr Matter took a piece of paper from his pocket and wrote down a name.

"Here," he said, handing it to me, "go see him. A former student of mine. His family owns the music store."

"Of course. That's where my father buys his pianos."

"Ask for Georg. Tell him you're one of my students. He'll give you the address of all the women conductors in Switzerland. I know there are two, possibly three. Then get in touch with them. Find out what it takes to become a conductor."

I thanked my teacher. I wouldn't be taking lessons anymore. I was eighteen, I had told my parents, and I'd had enough music lessons for a lifetime. Surprisingly, they agreed.

A few weeks after I passed my exams, I was summoned by the canton of Berne to take a home economics course, on account of my gender and my resident status there. I was not amused. Having just spent twelve years in school, I wasn't eager to set foot in a classroom again. And I certainly didn't want to learn about cooking and sewing, skills I considered totally useless since I was never, ever, going to be a *Hausfrau*. I fought the summons, maintained that I was only in Berne temporarily, I was going abroad, and anyway I shouldn't have to take part in this sort of training since I didn't even understand the language of instruction, Swiss German. My pleas fell on the deaf ears of Bernese bureaucrats.

I reported to the assigned school one morning, determined to sabotage the course. For starters I pretended not to understand a word of *Schwyzerdütsch*. The instructors, all female, had no choice but to speak to me in *Hochdeutsch* (High German). Then I led them to believe that I only understood a few words of German, so the instructors tried to speak to me in French. But their accent was thick: I professed not to understand their version of French.

Needless to say, I didn't make any friends. The girls in the course busied themselves with various chores, oblivious to my state of rebellion. Or perhaps they attributed this bad attitude to my being *Romande*. My staged ineptitude proved effective, however. Soon my comrades-in-arms were helping. I ended up doing very little cooking and absolutely no sewing.

We were told to make an article of clothing of our own design. Home Ec skills I lacked, but fashion design? That I could do. I drew an absurdly intricate pattern, knowing full well that I wouldn't be able to complete the assignment. One of the teachers took pity on me—or else she saw this as an opportunity to sew something a bit more exciting than the usual drab skirts. She agreed to help me make it. In fact, she did it all. My contribution was to hand her thread, needles, scissors and pins, as needed. Maman and I searched high and low in Berne's fabric stores to find the right material. A rather expensive piece of white *étoffe*, with satiny lining, was finally located and I began to look forward to going to school every day. What I visualized was a short evening gown with dramatic opening in the back, to be worn with or without a draped hood held in place by two long, crossed straps hanging loosely over the shoulders. The dress was spectacular. I think the teacher secretly enjoyed making it, although she complained that it would never be finished on time.

I brought it home and wore it once, I believe. To be honest, it was not the kind of creation you can wear more than once. Maman wasn't pleased to have spent money on a garment that now hung in the closet, gathering dust.

During that time another drama was unfolding at home. Grandpapa de Lausanne was dying of prostate cancer. My mother spent a lot of time at the Inselspital in Berne where he had been transferred to be in my father's care. Grandmaman de Lausanne moved in with us, sharing my room. She didn't take up a lot of space, but by God did she snore! How could such a loud noise, I wondered night after night, emanate from a gentle, fragile soul? Sadly, Grandpapa died in the spring of 1970. I had been too young to attend my other grandfather's funeral in Neuchâtel, so this was my first experience with the rituals of death. We had a private burial at the municipal cemetery of Pully, followed by a gathering of the family at Uncle Edouard's apartment in Lausanne.

Those were the cousins we didn't like. There had been, years before, bad blood between my father and Edouard. Papa didn't like his brother-in-law initially because he didn't come to my parents' wedding. My uncle was not yet married to Yolande and, as befitted the times, my parents invited him but not her. Edouard was offended that his future wife had not received an invitation and chose not to attend. Later, there was the story of the Greek vase. My grandfather had been given an urn as payment for services rendered; unaware of its value, he had brought it home, placed it on a table in the *salon* and forgotten all about it. Until my father, avid collector of antiques, commented on the beauty of the vase and confirmed its authenticity. Grandpapa de Lausanne, who was very fond of my father, immediately instructed his wife to give him the vase upon his death. But after my grandfather died, my uncle contested the legitimacy of the gift. Furious, Grandmaman went to see a lawyer. He came up with the idea of presenting my uncle with a steep bill for hospital expenses incurred as a result of my grandfather's illness (my father never charged his in-laws, of course, but Uncle Edouard was not privy to that bit of information). Grandmaman knew her son wouldn't be able to pay the bill. In the end, my uncle, faced with a dilemma of Greek proportions, renounced his claim to the vase, which remained in Papa's possession. The incident did nothing to endear Edouard to my father. On the contrary, contact between the families was severed permanently. Maman didn't mind too much, because she wasn't that close to her brother and had never cared for Yolande anyway.

Tante Yolande was French, snooty, and had the dubious distinction of having both a mother and a sister locked up in mental institutions somewhere in France. With her manicured nails, impeccable coiffure and affected style, she gave the impression of being descended from aristocratic stock. I suspect she was a peasant, just like us. Meanwhile, money was slipping through my uncle's fingers faster than he could say "Hey, I'm broke!" According to family lore, Uncle Edouard got in the habit of borrowing money from his father to pay for his wife's extravagant tastes. After Grandpapa passed away, Edouard tried, in vain, to continue the practice with his mother. And after his own mother died, he succeeded in swindling his sisters from a share of their inheritance, causing a colleague who knew him to remark:

"What he did was borderline legal."

Funny how children sometimes take on the feelings that their parents display towards other people. My brother and I made endless fun of Edouard and Yolande's three children: dowdy Bernadette (she already looked like an old maid at age ten), prickly Vincent (forever pursing his lips, which were thin to begin with), and Carole—well, she was the youngest of all the cousins, and we didn't really know her, but we disliked her on principle.

The other branch of the family consisted of my mother's sister, Gaby, her Swiss German husband, Adolphe, and their two children, Ariane and Philippe. I loved Uncle Adolphe, a jolly grandfather type, thirteen years older than my aunt, who always played with me and gave me treats. An industrialist from Zurich, he had met Gaby when she became his housekeeper. She had gone to Zurich to learn German and also, perhaps, to distance herself from her parents. Ill suited to the world of business, she seemed headed for the single life, when she upped and married her employer. Adolphe was kind, generous, and above all, accomodating. Unfortunately, many French-speaking families have a bias against acquiring a Swiss German relative through marriage. Our family was no exception. Grandmaman de Lausanne, way ahead of her time in so many respects, never accepted her son-in-law as a full member of the "clan." Despite evidence that he treated his wife very well indeed, enabling her to freely pursue her artistic interests, my grandmother held on to her stereotypes of Swiss Germans, primarily because of the way Adolphe spoke French. It didn't help matters that my aunt complained to her mother about her husband's shortcomings. Towards the end of her life, while occupying the comfortable flat Uncle Adolphe had thoughtfully offered her on the top floor of his apartment building, Grandmaman recognized her error in judgment.

I had a crush on my cousin Philippe. And I loved spending time with Ariane, a dark-haired beauty with Brigitte Bardot lips. Artistic, spirited, self-assured, Ariane set up window displays for Jelmoli, an upscale department store in Lausanne. She showed such promise as a *décoratrice* that her boss sent her to the flagship store in Zurich, where she moved shortly after her father's premature death. Uncle Adolphe, the owner of several properties, provided well for his family: Gaby got the apartment building in Pully, where she had lived for years; Ariane the house in Höngg near Zurich; and Philippe the villa in Arziers overlooking Lake Geneva.

Ariane, who enjoyed a close relationship with Grandpapa, was devastated by his death and nearly collapsed at the funeral. As soon as we arrived at Uncle Edouard's apartment I retreated to the secluded garden, where I was joined by Philippe. Sitting on a bench, drawing random shapes in the gravel at our feet, we mocked the forced cordiality of our cousins, reflected on the meaning of life, and shared our plans for the future—which included, for both of us, moving far, far away from Switzerland.

I woke up one day and told my mother I didn't want to go to university.
"What are you planning to do instead?"

"I want to go live on a farm."
Maman didn't blink.
"Okay, let's do some research."

We found an organization that matched up students who had a desire to farm and farmers in need of cheap labor during the summer holidays. I took the train, wearing the St. Christopher's cross that Maman had given me as a talisman, and headed north via Basel, Karlsruhe, Wiesbaden, Cologne, and finally Münster, where the farmer's wife picked me up. Theirs was no rickety old farm. It was a substantial property, with an impressive house attached to a large barn, several outbuildings, all of it surrounded by vast fields. There were herds of cows, as well as horses, pigs, ducks, chickens, dogs, cats. Also living on the farm were about twenty farmhands, to whom I was summarily introduced in the large, well-appointed kitchen upon arriving.

The farmer's wife struck me as a no-nonsense kind of woman. She showed me to my room, in a wing that was separate from the family quarters, and pointing at my outfit, suggested I change into something more suitable for farm work.

For about three weeks I did a variety of chores. First, the milking of the cows—not by hand as this was a high-tech operation, but with electric devices. The trick was to correctly place the contraption, a sort of four-legged octopus, on the cow's teats; the machine did the rest. Next came the tending of the pigs—not bad if you could stand the filth and the smell, although I confess the piglets, with their pink skin and curly tails, were kind of cute. What I really wanted to do, however, was to drive a tractor. First I had to prove myself, so I worked hard to show that I could take on any task. One morning after breakfast I was given a large key. This is where you drive the tractor, I was told. No further instructions. Off I went into the fields, tossing about on the tractor's seat, which was shaped like a spoon with holes. My job was to plough. It sure beat milking the cows or feeding foul-looking scraps to the pigs. Some of the farmhands were giving me looks, but I ignored them.

My room was at the end of a long hallway on the first floor of the hired help building. One night I awoke to the sound of a key being turned in my door from the outside. I sat up in bed, and asked, *"Wer ist da?"* ("Who is it?") I heard muted voices, suppressed laughter. I jumped out of bed and stood still, staring at the moving door handle. Suddenly, two men burst into the room, grinning. Too petrified to move, I stayed where I was, aware of the flimsiness of my nightgown. I raised my voice and said, *"Get out of here! Leave now!"* The men, clearly drunk, leered at me. One of them took a step in my direction. The other one, on the look-out, remained by the door. I began to scream *"Hilfe! Hilfe!"* The drunken farmhands turned around and left. The corridor was quiet. I knew there were other people occupying that floor, people who must have heard the commotion. A sleepy student emerged from his room and asked what was going on. When I told him, he said:

"Oh well, no harm done, go back to bed."

I wanted to take refuge in the farmer's private house, but that would have meant going outside in the dark and possibly running into those farmhands again. Still shaking, I secured the door and dragged a heavy wooden table in front of it. Even though it was warm I closed the window. I lay awake for the rest of the night.

Early next morning I went in search of the farmer's wife to tell her what happened. I expected her to be shocked and immediately reprimand and punish the guilty parties. She didn't seem overly concerned. She hadn't heard any noises during the night, she said. Was she accusing me of lying? We were standing in the kitchen, off to the side, while several students and farmhands—including the two culprits—were having breakfast at the long table. Every so often they threw glances our way, hoping to catch snippets of our conversation. The farmer's wife didn't believe me. Why would I make up such a story, I asked her. She found the whole thing farfetched. I stood there, unsure of what to do next. I wanted to call my mother, but calls were only for emergencies. Was this an emergency? The farmhands finished their meal and left, some of them smirking at me on their way out.

"I think it's best if you pack your bags and leave," said the farmer's wife, quietly.

"What?"

"We don't want any trouble. You never really belonged here, you know, you are a city girl."

I stared at her in disbelief.

"Someone will drive you to the station."

"But . . . they . . . they are the ones who should be . . . ." I didn't even know their names.

"Now if you'll excuse me, I have a lot to do."

In 1970 my brother was studying at the University of Zurich. He had transferred there to avoid having his father as a teacher at the University of Berne. His German girlfriend, also a medical student, rented a *Stöckli*—small cottage on a farm—in Niederwangen, a few kilometers from the capital. I had never visited her, but when I returned from Germany Maman talked to my brother who, in turn, spoke with his girlfriend about letting me stay at the cottage. Since she was spending the summer elsewhere, the *Stöckli* would be empty anyway. Her landlord, a hardy Bernese farmer, agreed to take me on as extra help for a few weeks.

The farmhouse was a modest structure with a pitched roof extending over the sides of the house. Red geraniums cascading from window boxes adorned its façade. Inside, there was a small, dark kitchen where the farmer, his wife and their grown son ate; a parlor used for formal occasions; two bedrooms and a bath. The attached barn housed a handful of cows, a couple of horses, a dog.

I was glad to be able to live in the cottage. It stood within view of the farmhouse, which made me feel safe, but gave me the privacy I craved. The place, decorated with warm colors and modern furniture, exuded a cozy, bohemian air. Every morning after breakfast, I walked over to the farm and started my chores. No high-tech milking machine here. I fed hay to the horses, picked potatoes, fetched fresh eggs, cleaned out the chicken coop. Lunch and dinner we all ate at the kitchen table—hearty meals of *Rösti* (shredded potatoes fried into a large pancake), sausages, homegrown vegetables. What did we talk about? I haven't a clue. The farmers only spoke *Schwyzerdütsch*, but somehow we managed to communicate.

Life on the farm turned out to be quite pleasant. Until, that is, I decided to throw a party. What a golden opportunity, I thought. I was finally living by myself, and the *Stöckli* looked quaint enough that I wouldn't be embarrassed to invite people over. Should I inform the farmer? Definitely wouldn't tell my brother or his girlfriend. Why bother them with such trivia? After all, the place would be tidied up afterwards. Excitement grew as I began to make a list.

When Herr Matter sent me to Georg, he didn't know—or maybe the crafty old devil did know—the effect that meeting would have on me. I walked into the store and asked for him. Which one, the father or the son? The son, I replied, hoping to have guessed right. While I waited, I took in my surroundings. Sounds of classical music wafted from the second floor where records (as in long-playing vinyl 33⅓ rpm recordings) were sold. The multi-floor building, in the heart of the Old Town, carried "Everything for Music" as its slogan promised. The clear-glass listening booths, where you could play LP's before making your selection, were eminently popular. Suddenly Georg—tall and slim with dark hair, white teeth contrasting nicely with his tan complexion—was there, smiling, offering his hand. Somewhat shakily I introduced myself in High German, and explained the reason for my visit. He nodded, still smiling, and switched to French, which he spoke fluently. I thanked him for his willingness to help. Not at all, came the answer, it would be a pleasure to satisfy such an unusual request. Would I be able to come back tomorrow for the information? Of course. We shook hands again and I left.

I found the man of my dreams, I wanted to shout. *He is handsome, obviously intelligent, speaks excellent French, and plays the piano. I'll marry him and have his babies, and together we'll play duets.* But for any of that to happen I had to make an impression, and there wasn't much time. I tried to imagine his private life. With killer looks like that, he must be a playboy. That meant tons of girlfriends, all more beautiful and sophisticated than I could ever hope to be. What if he was married? Please, don't let him be married! Unless . . . unless he was *unhappily* married.

As soon as I got home I ripped through my closet, looking for a suitable outfit. I didn't have a suitable outfit. What do you wear to tear a married man (if, in fact, he was a married man) away from his wife? What would I say to him? What if he forgot? What if he gave the information to one of the salespeople and I never saw him again? No, no, that couldn't happen. I spent hours fine-tuning my appearance, my entrance, my speech. Maman was too preoccupied with her father's illness to pay any attention.

When Georg and I met the following day, we seemed to have eyes only for each other. We chatted about music, our favorite composers, Herr Matter, Papa's Steinway—anything to prolong the bliss. A saleswoman interrupted our conversation; Georg was needed upstairs. Once again we shook hands and I wandered off in a daze.

In my mind I replayed the entire encounter: the words he spoke, the way he looked at me, the touching of our hands. Now that I had met him, how could I live without him? Life was cruel. Love was cruel. For this was love. Love for a man, not a boy like the others. But how could I ever hope to capture this man's heart?

I went home, sat at the piano and started to compose a tune. Composition, despite years of lessons at the Conservatory, was not my forte. After numerous revisions, I penned the finished product and titled it:

RAJMOHAN
Poème pour Piano Seul

The composition was dedicated, with a flourish, to Georg. I mailed the large envelope and waited for God to work His magic.

I come from a line of non-believers, or at least, non-practitioners. Grandmaman de Lausanne, born Catholic, suffered much abuse from her family and the local townsfolk when she married Grandpapa, a Protestant and thus, in their eyes, a heretic. She and all her children would rot in hell, they warned her.

Early in their marriage, Grandpapa said to his wife:

"If you can give me one good reason why I should convert to your religion, I will."

"I can't," Grandmaman replied, and that was the end of that.

When Maman got her first period at the age of thirteen, she became so enraged at the injustice of it all—this was long before the advent of tampons, when keeping the menstrual flow from soiling women's clothes greatly restricted their ability to play sports—that she willed herself to stop menstruating. She was furious with God. Up to that point, she had been a good girl who diligently studied the Bible and went to Sunday school. But how, she now asked herself, could a fair-minded God have made things so different for boys and for girls? Grandmaman took her to see a doctor, who assured her that her daughter's period would return on its own. And it did, a year and a half later.

Maman never entirely regained her faith after puberty. She was brought up as a Protestant since Grandmaman didn't care for the fanaticism of her fellow Catholics, but soon began to question the purpose of religion. A skeptic who didn't begrudge other people their own beliefs, she preferred to discuss the essence of God from a philosophical perspective.

On my father's side, religion may have been practiced, but I never witnessed it. While my parents insisted that their children attend Sunday school and be confirmed in the French-speaking Eglise Réformée de Berne, they didn't set foot in that church unless they had a very good reason to do so.

While I awaited destiny's hand, Grandpapa died.

Shortly after the funeral, I received a handwritten note from Georg, thanking me for my thoughtful, and flattering, composition. *Thanking* me? That was it? He wasn't going to whisk me off to his elegant Junkerngasse apartment (I had looked up his address in the phone book) and make endless love to me? Sorely disappointed, I decided that men were nothing but trouble. The way they led you on and had the gall to *thank* you after you'd given them a piece of your heart!

The party never materialized. Before I could finalize my plans, disaster, in the form of my livid brother, struck.

Somehow, JC had gotten wind of it.

The party would bring together people with a connection to music. A lofty notion, don't you think? Georg politely declined on the grounds that he was married. How much more humiliation could I take?

As it turns out, a lot more. My brother suddenly showed up at the *Stöckli*. He slammed my suitcase on the bed and packed it with a vengeance. According to him, I was nothing but a liar and a thief.

"What were you thinking," he kept shouting, "having a party in someone else's house? Someone kind enough to let you stay here! That's how you show your gratitude, by throwing a secret party?"

It was all aboveboard, I countered. Look, I even invited my piano teacher, how bad can that be?

"Now listen to me," he said, shutting the case and straightening his six-foot frame. "For the next four weeks you're going to live at the farmhouse with the *paysans*, and since you can't be trusted, they'll be keeping a very close eye on you, understood?"

I nodded.

"Okay, let's go."

How I hated him at that moment! Accusing me of having less-than-honorable intentions when all I wanted to do was throw a party for music lovers.

The farmers were waiting for us. JC carried the suitcase into the parlor, a minuscule room with just enough space for a narrow bed and a small table. Where was I supposed to hang up my clothes? What about the bathroom? I couldn't imagine sharing it with these yokels. I heard my brother give them last-minute instructions before he left. The farmer, his wife and their son stood there, glowering at me. How was I going to survive in this dump for a whole month?

When I called Maman to complain, she wasn't sympathetic. Siding with my brother, she suggested I do as I was told.

Another farming experiment gone sour. By the end of the summer, I had decided never to set foot on a farm again.

Upon returning to my parents' apartment in the city, I was asked by Papa what my plans were for the fall. In other words, what studies did I want to undertake? Problem was, I had no idea. Unlike my parents and JC, who knew what they wanted to study after their *gymnase*, I was confused. The more I told my father I wasn't sure, the more impatient he became. Tension between us grew to the point where we stopped communicating. I ate before he came home and hid in my room until he left for work.

Maman discussed possible courses of action. Having said "No" to many of her suggestions, I finally hit upon something intriguing: physiotherapy. I don't know what made me think of it. In order to matriculate at the school of my choice in Freiburg-im-Breisgau, however, I first had to work in a hospital. Maman got into high gear and started making inquiries. An Oxford don, friend of my parents, pulled some strings and I was accepted as a nurse's aide at the Nuffield Orthopaedic Centre for a three-month internship to begin in October.

Sometime in September I approached my father while he was relaxing in the *fumoir* after lunch. Maman was in Lausanne, helping Grandmaman deal with the aftermath of her husband's death. Eager to share my good news, I walked up to him and announced:

"Papa, I know what I want to do."

He beamed at me (when he was pleased, he had an enchanting smile).

"Oh yes? What is it?"

"I want to become a physiotherapist."

The smile vanished, replaced by a frown. He stood up, as if he might not have heard properly.

"What?"

"I'm going to be a physiotherapist."

"My daughter, a masseuse?" he spat out the word. "Never!"

I stood still, frightened by his outburst. Then I fled to my room where I packed my two red suitcases. As soon as I heard the front door slam, signaling Papa's departure—as well as his displeasure—I called my mother up. Plans were immediately set in motion for me to leave for England.

The next day I told my father, *"J'en ai marre! Je m'en vais."*

Chapter Two: ENGLAND

Ruby's Restaurant was started by my great-uncle Gustave in the seaside town of Cliftonville, near Margate, in the 1940's. According to family lore, Gustave left Switzerland at sixteen to seek his fortune in England. He washed dishes, scrubbed floors, and learned the fine art of cooking in some of London's best kitchens. Years later he found a position at a hotel in Margate and, subsequently, was able to fulfill his dream of owning a restaurant. An air of mystery and intrigue surrounded Uncle Gustave. He liked to drink, which would explain his rosy cheeks. He had a weakness for women (he married, was widowed, had numerous liaisons, carried on a long and stormy relationship with a woman who worked for him, and didn't leave any known heirs). He loved fast cars, especially Jaguars. But what truly defined him was his passion for food. In the kitchen at Ruby's he developed a following, a loyal clientele of English folks who loved his cuisine, not to mention his larger-than-life personality. My great-uncle was the epitome of the *bon vivant*. Sadly, he died before I could sample his cooking.

Gustave was one of Grandpapa de Neuchâtel's nine siblings. Life at the turn of the century for their poor, widowed mother wasn't easy; to feed her large brood, she sold homegrown produce at the local market in La Neuveville. Still, it took guts for Gustave to emigrate to a country whose language and culture were totally unfamiliar to him, without a *sou* to his name. I've always been fascinated by tales of relatives who went to live abroad. What possessed them to leave, when others would never even consider such a step? One of Gustave's sisters moved to South America. Another, Esther, traveled quite a bit as a children's governess. On my paternal grandmother's side, a great-aunt settled in Casablanca with her

Swiss husband. Another one, Georgette, spent her entire life in the South of France. Because I had met Gustave—very briefly when I was three or four—and seen photographs of him frolicking on an English beach with Maman and JC, he was the one who intrigued me the most. His journey across the Channel, apprenticeship in London, alcoholism, womanizing, talent as a chef—that was the stuff of juicy novels.

After Gustave died, one of his sous-chefs, John Giraud, bought the place. Banking on the restaurant's established reputation, he kept the name and continued its tradition of offering superb food in pleasant surroundings.

My mother kept in touch with the Girauds. Once a year they came to Switzerland to meet with their banker. Bubbly, girlish Margaret nicely counterbalanced John, who could be gruff and moody. By the time I knew them they were a middle-aged couple with no children—but a boxer named Jenny—and a Jag in the driveway. The house in Cliftonville, situated on a corner lot on Northdown Road, only a few minutes' walk from the Queen's Promenade, was a two-storied, detached brick property with a small fenced-in garden in back. The restaurant occupied the first floor while the Girauds' private accommodations took up the second floor. The lower floor was decidedly masculine; the upper, utterly feminine, with a pink leitmotiv of fluffy pillows, lacy curtains, and plush wall-to-wall carpeting. I relished Margaret's chintzy décor simply because it was so different from that to which I was accustomed. Downstairs was all polished wood, burgundy leather armchairs and crisp, white linen tablecloths. Food was showcased here, not furniture. To enter the restaurant you had to go through the bar and lounge area, which encouraged patrons to sip a sherry or gin and tonic before sitting down to eat. Margaret and I always sat at the same table and ordered whatever we fancied. My favorite dessert, or pudding, a warm apple crumble with custard, didn't look like much when it arrived in a plain white bowl, but one spoonful of the heavenly concoction always sent me howling for more.

Margaret, a born schmoozer, liked to walk around the dining room and make small talk with diners, remembering their names, ensuring they were satisfied, inquiring about their health (since most of the clientele had reached the age when that becomes a daily preoccupation), introducing me as Gustave's great-niece from Switzerland, with one of her trademark winks. The kitchen was John's fiefdom. He ruled it like a despot, shouting orders as well as insults at the kitchen staff—never up to par, in his opinion—while creating culinary masterpieces to be savored by unsuspecting customers on the other side of the swing door. At times John's bellowing voice erupted from the kitchen, making Margaret flush with embarrassment. I followed her advice and avoided the entire food preparation area during lunch and dinner. John, she warned me, was even more impossible there than at home.

Cliftonville is where I took refuge before embarking on my internship in Oxford. There were many fringe benefits to staying with the Girauds. For one, they doted on me, their surrogate, Continental daughter. It seemed like the perfect relationship: they could spoil me rotten without fear of inflicting long-lasting damage, as they knew my presence in their midst to be temporary; and I was only too glad to help my adoptive parents with the restaurant and the dog because they were so refreshingly lenient, with no expectations except that I should enjoy myself.

For another, I ate exceedingly well. When the restaurant was closed John whipped up delicious meals for the three of us in the small kitchen upstairs, which we ate on tray tables while watching telly. How much better could life be?

Jenny was the dog I could never have at home, a tan boxer with a streak of white on her chest, full of energy yet docile when it was demanded of her. Every day I took her for long walks on the seafront promenade. This was the seventies, when owners were not required by law to pick up after their dogs, or keep them on a leash, so I could stroll without a care in the world, only restraining Jenny when she got the urge to chase after birds. The Girauds' only child, she had many privileges: she slept in their room, where she commandeered a luxurious bed strewn with numerous toys, was bathed and brushed weekly, and ate first-class leftovers from the kitchen. In return she placed slobbering kisses on the faces of her masters at every opportunity (I qualified as interim mistress).

As if all of the above weren't enough to keep me enthralled, I acquired two new skills along the way. I learned to tend bar, courtesy of John and Margaret, who taught me how to identify different bottles of liquor, measure the right amount into the proper glasses, use the mixer, add the odd olive, lemon twist or maraschino cherry, pour beer like a pro. And last, but not least, I perfected my English. That was, after all, one of the reasons I had come to England.

Those weeks in Cliftonville were glorious. My life revolved around gastronomy with John, shopping with Margaret, seaside walks with Jenny. The town of Margate, a resort since Victorian times, is situated on the Isle of Thanet (which actually was an island back in the days of the Roman occupation). The seafront is characterized by low chalk cliffs and beaches with rock pools; cockles, whelks and other mollusks abound, a source of delight for children carrying pails and nets. From Cliftonville it is a short distance to Foreness Point, the most south-easterly part of Britain. Margate and its tacky amusement pier had seen better days, I'm sure, but Cliftonville, with its Regency crescents, leafy streets, well-clipped hedges, gave off a sense of quiet content. The picturesque promenade along the sea, above the cliffs, attracted both locals and holiday-makers. This being the

North Sea, sunbathing tended to be uncommon and arrived at accidentally rather than deliberately, and the water temperature remained cool, even in summer. One constant on British beaches, whether it be Torquay (fondly referred to as the capital of the English Riviera) or Brighton, seems to be the ever present breeze, hence the striped windbreaks that dot its sandy stretches.

There was one park in Cliftonville that Margaret favored because of its lovely walled rose garden. We often walked there with Jenny and sat on a bench, breathing in the heady fragrance. Margaret, quite tall with a slight hump, had a taste for pretty things: flowers, the color pink, jewelry, frou-frou designs and dainty knickknacks. On shopping expeditions we behaved like schoolgirls. Before returning home we'd stop at the local bakery where she introduced me to Battenberg, a marzipan-covered sponge cake with alternating layers of pink and yellow.

A hopeless romantic and resident matchmaker, Margaret was forever trying to set me up with an English Prince Charming. None of it paid off, but it was nice to have her make such a fuss. She openly complained about her husband's smoking, his temper, his coarseness, the lack of romance in their marriage. For his part, John, still a handsome man in the Jean-Paul Belmondo mold, seemed exasperated by Margaret's constant nagging. I found their banter entertaining. On occasion John spent Sunday evening with his pals, leaving Margaret and me to fix our own dinner. Margaret could not cook to save her life. Her idea of a nice supper was baked beans on toast (to this day I enjoy the dish, which always reminds me of her).

On his days off John took me for rides in his beloved car. Ruby's closed after lunch on Sunday and reopened at noon on Tuesday. Mondays we would get supplies in neighboring towns, and visit other restaurants in the area. We often stopped for lunch at small inns hidden away on narrow country lanes. Inevitably, John and Margaret knew the owner or the chef, and our meals were divine. Driving around the Kentish countryside I came upon many attractions: thatched cottages and half-timbered public houses with names like The Cock and Bull, The Rose and Crown, The Admiral Nelson; coastal paths running along steep cliffs; charming little towns like Broadstairs, at the very tip of the Thanet promontory, which overlooks Viking Bay and where Charles Dickens, a regular visitor, finished *David Copperfield;* the beaches at Stone Bay and Botany Bay; Deal and its oddly shaped castle (not that we ever visited historic sites, thank God); Sandwich, named for a certain earl whose main claim to fame was that he invented the sandwich, a bit of meat slapped between two slices of bread, as a quick snack during a 24-hour game of cards (John told the story every time we passed through town, despite his wife's insistence that we knew about the bloody earl already); Canterbury, of pilgrim fame and home to England's first cathedral; Dover and its celebrated white cliffs, as well as its sole, where John picked me up when I first arrived from Calais by ferry.

It was, therefore, with trepidation that I prepared to take leave of my home away from home. The Girauds brought me to the station one morning in late October to board the London train. John gave me money for the cab fare from Victoria Station to Paddington Station.

"You come back and visit us very soon, you hear?" Margaret said, embracing me.

John carried my suitcases onto the train and placed them in the overhead rack.

"There," he said, "you'll be fine here."

I nodded.

"Don't be a stranger."

We hugged one last time and the train pulled away.

What I clearly remember from that first dreary, drizzly day in Oxford was being hungry and desperately looking for a suitable place to eat. The little money I had was to last me three months. After I sat down in a bland self-service eatery, I lost my appetite and began to question my sanity. Why had I left home? Or Cliftonville? What in the world was I doing in Oxford? I didn't know a soul, the food on my plate didn't exactly blow me away, and it was dark at three in the afternoon. I didn't recall such gloomy weather in Kent. As a matter of fact, when I conjured up images of Kent, all I saw was sunshine, carefree days. My four-o'clock appointment with the don, arranged through Maman's efforts, is what kept me from going back to Cliftonville.

I tried not to look like a tourist, but the way in which I pored over the map of Oxford must have given me away. The city was easy to navigate and soon I found myself in front of an imposing Tudor adjacent to one of the colleges. A middle-aged couple, tall and patrician, welcomed me into their stately home. Over tea we chatted about Oxford, my parents, my internship at Nuffield.

It was getting late. I thanked my hosts for their hospitality and walked back to the station to collect my luggage.

The Nuffield Orthopaedic Centre, a large complex consisting of several low buildings connected by footpaths, sat on a small hill in Headington, a ten-minute bus ride from the center of town. I asked the driver where to get off, and dragged my red suitcases towards the main entrance. This was going to be my home for the next three months. After I checked in at the front desk, a nurse showed me to my Spartan quarters. I was given a nursing auxiliary's uniform, a light yellow cotton frock with starched white cap. My hair at the time was long; I was told to keep it tied back during work. I unpacked my belongings and made my way to the staff dining room, located in another building. The food turned out to be the best thing about Nuffield. Clearly, rumors as to the terrible state of English cuisine were exaggerated. The cafeteria was airy, modern, spotless, and I looked forward to every meal. Like a pack rat I stuffed my pockets with pre-wrapped mini-portions of Double Gloucester, Cheshire, Red Leicester, crackers, biscuits, and puddings for late night snacks in my room.

Food became the running theme of my stint at Nuffield. I quickly came to the realization that working in a hospital was not for me. But I found a purpose. Twice a day, mid-morning and mid-afternoon, I wheeled in a trolley of coffee and tea, scones, crumpets, jam, cakes and sandwiches for the patients. I drove that trolley like a convertible, and the faithful could hear me coming down the hall by the clatter of cups and saucers. I took my time serving them, indulging their desire for a certain pastry or biscuit, chatting with them, making them laugh. The rest of the day was spent handing out plastic bedpans and removing them after they had been used, adjusting beds, fluffing pillows, bringing supplies to the nurses (nursing auxiliaries didn't get to rub elbows with those gods of medicine, doctors). The lowest point occurred one day when a frail, elderly woman began to vomit something greenish. I fled to the loo where I hid until it was time to bring around the tea trolley.

I made few acquaintances among the staff, but befriended an Indian girl, also an aide. Together we roamed around town on our days off, trying to make the most of our meager wages. We browsed through bookstores, window shopped along the High Street, watched crews of rowers practice their skill in perfect synchronization on the River Cherwell, sipped hot chocolate in smoky coffee shops filled with students. There was a boutique on Cornmarket that sold funky, inexpensive clothes; I went there often, rarely to purchase, mostly to look and to talk with the salesgirl, who was about my age. One evening towards the end of our internship, my Indian friend and I decided to treat ourselves to a fancy dinner—by that we meant a sit-down dinner in a proper restaurant with actual waiters, as opposed to the self-service cafeterias and pubs we normally frequented.

It didn't take me long to feel completely at home in this fair city dominated by the university's spires and towers. Soaking up the academic and cultural atmosphere, while remaining on the sidelines as a working girl, suited me just fine. I even went to a museum, the Ashmolean, of my own free will. During the day, gowned students bicycled through the streets, on their way, I imagined, to a lecture given by a stern professor. I took shortcuts through the colleges' quads, walking past immaculate grounds where faculty and budding scholars conversed. Funny thing is, whenever I mention that I lived in Oxford in the seventies, people immediately assume

I was a student there. I enjoy watching their reaction when I tell them I wasn't studying in the hallowed halls of Balliol or Magdalen College at all, but cleaning bedpans at the local hospital. Somehow, living in historic Oxford made the cleaning of bedpans more bearable.

On the one hand, I was relieved to have discovered, sooner rather than later, that I wasn't cut out to work in a hospital. On the other, since my plan to become a physiotherapist had fallen through, what was I going to do now? I was supposed to go back to Switzerland, but didn't feel like it. The answer came by way of an unexpected offer. The mother of one of the patients on my ward took me aside and asked if I would be interested in working as an au-pair for her daughter after she was discharged from the hospital. Charlotte and her husband, a doctor with a new practice in Cheltenham, had recently moved to the Cotswolds with their two little girls, aged two and four. I finished my internship without incident, received a glowing recommendation from the matron, and in January, packed my suitcases again. This time I was headed for a house on Banbury Road, where Charlotte's parents lived. I spent one night there, and the next day Charlotte, her husband, their daughters and the dog, a large Airedale terrier scrunched up in the back of the station wagon, said goodbye to Oxford and drove west.

The Cotswolds, notwithstanding the season, were a revelation: sleepy hamlets nestled among gentle hills, stone walls crisscrossing endless meadows, an ancient wool mill by a river's edge, sheep wandering on twisty country lanes, the distinctive twin chimneys and mullioned windows of century-old cottages, small market towns with their quaint shops and traditional tea rooms. I had loved Kent, and more recently Oxford, but this—this was the England of picture postcards. After two hours' drive we arrived at a grey stone cottage in Sheepscombe, near Painswick. The Airedale leapt from the car and barked excitedly. Another dog to take on walks.

My accommodations, an enormous bedroom with adjoining bath, were situated above a workshop where Charlotte's husband liked to tinker on weekends. Two windows looked over a small patio, at the center of which stood an old well. The cottage was set in the middle of an ample, sloping garden. Pleasantly surprised, I began to unpack.

Later, Charlotte showed me around the house and went over my responsibilities. First and foremost, I would take care of the girls: getting them up and dressed in the morning, feeding them, entertaining them, taking them for walks with the dog in the nearby forest, giving them their bath in the evening, tidying up their room. I was also expected to help in the kitchen and, on occasion, cook a meal.

"I'm afraid my cooking isn't very good," I warned her.

"Don't worry, nothing fancy. We're not talking gourmet meals. Just some spaghetti and sauce, that sort of thing."

A comfortable routine set in. Daddy went to work in the morning. I minded the girls while Mummy, still recovering from her surgery, took naps and puttered around the house until dinnertime, at which point Daddy returned from work and we all sat down to eat. Charlotte wasn't a bad cook. Her food would never match John's, but it didn't fit the soggy-vegetables-and-dry-pot-roast cliché either. I learned to make a few dishes in that kitchen, a mixture of English and Italian fare.

I got along well with the girls, although the oldest was a handful. A wee plump, full of mischief and prone to tantrums, she often played me against her mother. In contrast, her younger sister was a breeze: sweet and affectionate, always willing to follow my lead.

The house looked like an authentic eighteenth-century cottage on the outside, with all mod cons inside. Several narrow passages led to small rooms on different levels, reached by a winding staircase. Nooks and crannies beckoned everywhere, and low, beamed ceilings gave the place a cozy feel. Three fireplaces kept the damp, cold winter air at bay. The décor, with its yellow and blue patterned prints, was cheerful.

On my days off I explored the surrounding towns of Cirencester, Stroud, Bibury, Cheltenham, Gloucester. Conveniently, the local bus stopped right up the road from the cottage. The fact that the route was most circuitous, including every possible stop along the way, didn't matter. The ride itself was an adventure, and I sat, content to watch the scenery and listen in on conversations between other riders. Once at my destination I walked around, perhaps treating myself to a cream tea (warm scones with strawberry jam and clotted cream), basking in my freedom for a few hours.

When she hired me, Charlotte asked if I could drive. "I can drive," I told her, "but I don't have a permit." In Switzerland Maman had encouraged me to drive her Mini in empty parking lots. But when it came time to take the written test, I failed. A few weeks after my arrival in Sheepscombe, Charlotte offered to pay for me to take the driving test in Cheltenham and get a UK driver's license. I practiced a few times in her car, also a Mini, until I felt comfortable with the right-hand drive, and passed the test with flying colors—and flying I was when I rounded that corner, said the examiner, an older gentleman who was sufficiently swayed by what he called my "charming accent" to omit it in his report.

The village of Sheepscombe consisted of a handful of houses huddled together at the bottom of a small valley, with a few cottages scattered on the surrounding slopes. A small stream ran through the hamlet; a tiny church, pub, and two or three shops completed the picture. It was nice enough to be able to get a few supplies within walking distance, even if it took a good half hour.

When I expressed a longing to play the piano, which I hadn't done in months, Charlotte called a retired couple, owners of a grand piano, who lived on the other side of the village. They were more than willing to have someone bring their unused instrument back to life. Once or twice a week I tucked my sheet music (I always travel with a few favorites, just in case) under my arm and walked over to their house, a downhill stroll from the cottage on a tortuous road, followed by a steep hike to their house, all of it to be retraced at the end of practice. I didn't mind. These delightful people welcomed me with open arms, insisting I could come and play anytime I wished. If they weren't home, a key would be left by the door. But they were always home when I got there. After the initial greetings, they retreated to another part of the house or the garden. The piano sat in a large living room with bay windows that looked over the outlying valley. Tea with biscuits or slices of cake was served after my sessions, a ritual I especially enjoyed.

During one of my trips to Cirencester, I went into a photo shop to have some pictures developed. The man behind the counter told me I should be a model. (What a thing to say to a young, vulnerable girl.) Next he proposed dinner (impossible), or at least lunch (maybe), well then coffee (okay), and offered to take my picture for free. I agreed to pose in the back of the shop, and when I came back a few days later I couldn't believe the results. He had taken black-and-white close-ups of my sober face staring into the camera: hair pulled back starkly, fake beauty spot on the cheek, pouty lips. They reminded me of those Warhol portraits I had seen in art galleries. The photographer handed me two poster-size enlargements that he carefully rolled up in a cardboard tube. He suggested taking more pictures. As flattered as I was by his attention (he was, after all, a fully grown man), I was also nervous. I thanked him for the photos, took the bus home, and never went back.

I had turned nineteen at Nuffield, and was most eager to have a boyfriend. But that guy wasn't going to be the one.

The girls and I took the Airedale for daily walks in the woods near the house. Since my primary exposure to the species had been with Jenny, I didn't know much about the male variety. One morning after breakfast I said playfully to the dog:

"Let's go for a walk, okay? Do you want to go for a nice, long walk in the forest?"

Well, did he ever. I finished loading up the dishwasher, grabbed a leash from the hook next to the door, and as I turned to put it on, noticed a pink protuberance glistening under his belly. That thing was huge. In a mild panic, I called Charlotte. When she came running down the stairs, I pointed at the mystery ailment. Charlotte took one look and laughed.

"He's not sick, that's his penis!"

"His . . . his . . . penis?" I asked, incredulous.

The anticipation of a walk had aroused the poor chap. Even the girls, who had followed their mother and now stood giggling in the middle of the kitchen, knew about dog anatomy. I giggled too, to mask my embarrassment.

Spring arrived, bringing with it an explosion of flowers—snowdrops, crocuses, daffodils, bluebells—and the burgeoning of an idea. Life had been blissful in my fairytale cottage, but while I was changing a diaper one afternoon, the urge to do something a little more cerebral hit me.

Chapter Three: SWITZERLAND

*I*n May 1971, for the modest fee of 151 Swiss Francs (thanks to state-subsidized higher education), I enrolled at the University of Basel to study psychology.

Relations with my parents had deteriorated because I hadn't returned to Switzerland right after my internship. Even Maman seemed angry.

In April, after crossing the Channel, I had boarded the Calais-to-Basel train and, on impulse and without my parents' knowledge, landed at the lavish home of acquaintances of Papa's—the very same couple I had been dragged to see after the thwarted party—on the outskirts of Basel. My gracious hosts offered me dinner and a bath, after which they insisted I contact my parents to let them know where I was. Reluctantly, I dialed the number in St. Luc where I knew to find them. A brief conversation ensued, and it was agreed that I would come up the next day. I arrived at the chalet, not by postal bus, which is how you arrive when you don't have a car, but in a private automobile driven by a mechanic from a gas station in Sierre, at the foot of the Val d'Anniviers. Papa and Maman were furious. They offered to pay the driver, who gallantly refused; as soon as he left they turned towards me and demanded an explanation. The scowl on their faces was incomprehensible. Weren't they happy to see me after all this time?

Tension at the chalet was palpable. I told my parents I was ready to go to university, and was glad they didn't insist I study at the University of Berne. When I mentioned what I planned on studying, Papa's face fell. For him, psychology—anything starting with the prefix *psych* was automatically suspect—was a nebulous field that would never amount to a science, therefore an unworthy subject. But at least I was going to college, so he went along with the program.

Meanwhile, my parents were formulating a plan of their own. I was handed a so-called contract, the rules and conditions for my being able to study in Basel. It covered everything from a strict monthly budget to the type of accomodations (living with a family, as opposed to being on my own) they would pay for during my studies. The contract infuriated me, even though I doubted its validity in a court of law. I rebelled at the very notion of having such a document drawn up between parents and children, in spite of Maman's assurances that it was for my own good. I was especially annoyed at her, for it was her signature that appeared on the piece of paper. No matter how many times she told me that my father was equally in favor of the contract, I didn't believe her. Unbeknown to me, Maman had asked Papa to add his signature to hers, but he refused. So she gave him an ultimatum: If you don't sign it, I will leave you.

Our understanding was that I would go to Basel and stay at the youth hostel while I looked for a place to live. When I had found a suitable room, Maman would come and see for herself. I was motivated to find something quickly because I didn't like the hostel—filled, as it was, with cheerful backpackers enjoying the sights while I had to attend to the tedious business of finding lodgings. After a fruitless two-day search around the city, I rang the doorbell at 32 Steinengraben, a large townhouse not far from the university.

Frau Eichele was a widow with four children, three of whom lived with her—Matthias, age six, Katharina, age eight, and sixteen-year-old Lukas. Her oldest daughter, married, had moved away. Two boarders occupied the top floor, where a third room had just become available. The short, plump landlady beamed when she discovered I was going to be a psychology student.

"The room is yours. I would have liked my daughter to become a psychologist."

Not only did I get a room, but I was given one in a privileged part of the second floor, the family floor, instead of the third floor. Frau Eichele, in acquiring a new boarder, had gotten herself an extra daughter.

My room at Steinengraben became my realm. I used Grandmaman de Lausanne's old upright, complete with adjustable brass candle holders, to divide the space into living and sleeping quarters. A mattress on the floor behind the piano and Frau Eichele's glass-paneled armoire turned into my bedroom. A low bookshelf under the windowsill, enhanced by an ornate iron railing, made up the food prep area, where a variety of teas, brewed with the help of a portable heating coil, could be sampled in unmatched mugs, along with numerous cookies, salty snacks and chocolate bars. A red

Persian rug covered the wood floor, my preferred sitting area. The walls were lined with eclectic artifacts: one of my giant posters from England; quotes from philosophers I admired; bits of animal skins; photographs of a little boy peeing (what would Freud have to say about that?); postcards gleaned from various art museums; a sheet of paper with the words GETTING READY FOR THE US '72; colorful prints of Paris landmarks; attempts at Chinese calligraphy. Hanging on the back of the door was an assortment of sisal shoulder bags I had, for some reason, crocheted myself. Dozens of empty ochre-colored glass containers, testament to my consumption of yogurt, sat in a neat row on top of the piano. The ceiling, painted bright red with a contrasting white frieze running along its perimeter, gave the room a suitably unconventional touch.

My first semester course load included Intro to Psychology, General Psychology, Intro to Philosophy, a Philosophy of Education seminar, History of Composition, Ethnological Musicology, a Music seminar, Italian. By American standards, that may seem like an awful lot of classes. But I don't recall taking any exams, or even writing a paper. The main emphasis was on attending lectures, taking copious notes, and keeping up with assigned readings.

I settled happily in Frau Eichele's big house. Loved my freedom to come and go as I pleased. As second-floor occupant, I had full use of the kitchen downstairs where I occasionally heated up simple foods, as well as the huge family bathroom, which I regularly stank up with funky depilatory creams. The large window in my room faced one of many venerable trees dotting the broad avenue. I relished the sight of that loyal, steady friend, whose fate would bring about a most unexpected turn of events in the ensuing months.

From the moment I arrived in Basel I spoke *Hochdeutsch*, not *Schwyzerdütsch*. I didn't think I knew the latter well enough to make myself understood. But more importantly, I hated the way Swiss German sounded. One advantage of not speaking the local dialect was that people assumed I didn't understand what was being said. In reality, I understood a fair amount, notwithstanding the fact that there are countless vernaculars in the German part of Switzerland, each varying according to region. For instance, in Basel (Basu to the initiated) people tend to use a lot of *u* (as in the English *foot*) sounds, whereas in Berne they speak with a broad *ä* (as in *mad*) and in Zurich they favor *ü* (as in *hue*). Thus you end up with *Basudütsch* in Basel, *Bärndütsch* in Berne, *Züridütsch* in Zurich, and so on. I felt a bit like a spy, speaking *Hochdeutsch,* which elicited a response in High German, yet being able to figure out what people said around me. I never came clean, not even to my adopted family. It was much more fun to play linguistic games and remain the outsider. In all fairness, classes were taught in High German, and since there was a sizable foreign student population at the university, I didn't stand out by speaking High rather than Swiss German.

My love of everything foreign was reflected in the friendships I developed with Claudia, a chain-smoking, bleached blonde from Germany I met in one of my classes, and Sandra, a fast-talking Brazilian with whom I worked briefly at the post office to earn extra money. Sandra was a few years older, and married to a Swiss musician named Jean-Paul.

And of course, there were boys, plenty of boys.

With my parents' blessing (anything of a musical nature would have induced their blessing), I started to take violin lessons with an eccentric teacher in a leafy suburb of Basel. One of his protégés, a striking young man with jet black hair and long sideburns, became a fixture at 32 Steinengraben. Mario, a student at the university, was of Portuguese descent and endowed with endless patience. He showed me how to hold the bow properly, where to position my fingers, indulged my whim to try a passage, from the Franck Violin and Piano Sonata in A Major, which was way beyond my ability. To Frau Eichele's delight, we often played our instruments in my room where, in exchange for musical guidance, I offered him tea and conversation. Ours was a strictly platonic relationship, as I had my sights set on one sexy Hungarian.

János and I met one morning on our way to psychology class. I was climbing the narrow, circular steps to a classroom located on the top floor of an old-fashioned building as he came barreling down the stairs. We bumped into each other. Not one to waste time, he informed me that class had been canceled, and would I have coffee with him since we had two hours to kill? We strolled over to the cafeteria and talked at length, all the while sizing each other up. János, on the short side but well-built, was a fine specimen—a combination of unabashed virility, quick temper and disarming charm. He and his mother, with whom he lived in a modest apartment near Allschwilerplatz, had arrived in Basel in 1956 as refugees from the Hungarian Revolution.

Angelika, a second-year law student in Munich, and I had kept in touch since graduating from Mont-Olivet. When she came to visit during that first semester, I was excited to introduce her to my new boyfriend. The three of us went out to dinner; after a while, I noticed that János seemed far too interested in my girlfriend. So I imbibed, with rather messy consequences. János and Angelika carried me home and put me to bed. When I awoke the next morning, I knew with certainty that I would never get drunk again. Not long thereafter, I tried smoking. In the space of two short weeks I puffed on Benson & Hedges cigarettes, thin little cigars named Meccarillos, and a pipe, only to conclude, amid much coughing, that I didn't like any of them. That ended my brief experimentation with toxic substances.

Looking for a tennis partner on the university bulletin board one lazy afternoon, I was approached by someone in search of the same. Sandro, who hailed from Ticino, was an alumnus, a practicing chemist, and the nicest person you could ever meet. He drove a sports car, was a licensed pilot, and was willing to give me anything my little heart desired. Unfortunately, I didn't desire him. But we became good friends.

On the academic front, I was becoming disenchanted with the theoretical slant of my psychology classes. I had expected discussions of real-life situations, but all we ever did was analyze what the analysts put forward. I began to toy with the idea of switching to law—I could picture myself arguing a case with flourish in the courtroom, defending the innocent, the downtrodden, the poor. I skipped some classes and to supplement my allowance, worked as a truck dispatcher, a receptionist in an art gallery, a babysitter.

That summer I had a fling with an English law student I really, really liked. Martin and I met at tennis when we were paired as doubles partners, and even though he wasn't particularly handsome, there was something about him I found irresistible. I can't think what that might have been (he did look good in tennis whites), for he was average in every way. Martin shared an apartment near Spalentor with a fellow Brit who had conveniently decamped for the holidays, giving us all the privacy we needed. One day I bought a picnic lunch that ended up costing a fortune (I was trying to impress him with my worldly ways). At the gourmet store I splurged on a selection of cheeses, pâtés, exotic fruits and pastries; I even brought a bottle of wine, although I wasn't planning to drink any. The air filled with promise, I laid out the food on his balcony and figured it was money well spent. After dessert we retreated to Martin's room and kissed. I took off my top, sat on his narrow bed and waited. Martin stood in the middle of the room, unable to move. I couldn't understand why he wasn't taking advantage of me.

"I think you'd better go," he said.
"Why? What's the matter?"
He hesitated.
"I don't think we should do this."
"But . . . I thought you liked me!"
Silence.

Mortified, I put my top back on, picked up my bag and left. The last thing I wanted to do was to go home and cry. I would walk off my fury. On Nadelberg in the *Altstadt* I passed an art supply store and went in. That's what I'll do, I thought, paint my sorrow away. I picked out a foldable easel, small canvas, palette, three tubes of paint and two brushes. Short of cash (because of my extravagance earlier that day), I begged the salesman to hold everything until I returned from the bank with more Francs. That evening, I went to sleep staring at an unmitigated disaster—I didn't know oil took so long to dry. Later in the week, I went back to the art shop and asked for quick-drying paint. The three acrylic paintings that emerged in quick succession were all abstract and indicative of a range of moods: black and white (doom and gloom); black and yellow (there is hope); red and orange (fiery passion).

I never spoke to Martin again, and was relieved to hear he had gone back to England before the new term started.

The relationship with my parents was on the mend, or so I thought. When I went to Berne at the end of the summer to tell them I wanted to study law instead of psychology, they flipped out. Within days I was dispatched to a well-known psychiatrist in Zurich. My fickleness was cause for alarm. It was easier for my parents to think of me as mentally ill than merely confused. Confusion had no place in a family of overachievers. Just to spite Maman, who accompanied me to make sure I didn't bail out, I was deliberately rude and uncooperative with the doctor. Nevertheless, he told my mother after the session that I was perfectly normal. Vindicated, I now had the upper hand.

In November 1971 I matriculated again at the University of Basel, this time as a law student. I took Roman Private Law, Law of Contracts, Fundamentals of the Civil Code, Public Law, Legal Procedure, Fiscal Law, and Criminology. Excited at the prospect of dealing with a subject that would be so much more tangible and coherent than psychology, I threw myself into my studies.

It wasn't long before I got distracted by a tall, blond, good-looking student in Public Law. I made a bet with Brigitte that I could get his attention, and after several less-than-subtle attempts, succeeded in securing a date. Christian, it turns out, was German. Brigitte didn't think his brains matched his physique, but I enjoyed his company, though secretly bemoaned the fact that he had no sense of humor.

During Christmas break I took the train to Belgium and met up with Angelika in Liège. We stayed at the apartment of a friend of hers in a run-down neighborhood. It was bitter cold, the city was dull, and the locals didn't seem too friendly. I perked up somewhat when I discovered *chocolatiers* and *pâtisseries* at every corner. Angelika's friend was pleasant enough, but the entire weekend was a flop: we didn't do anything except drive around in his beat-up 2CV. To warm ourselves and stave off hunger—the fridge was bare, Angelika and I had to supply our own food—we stopped at stands selling warm *gaufres* (waffles) and *pommes frites* (French fries) with mayonnaise.

Little did I know then that I would relocate twice to Belgium with my future husband.

* * *

In January 1972 the city of Basel announced that the trees on Steinengraben were going to be taken down: the avenue needed widening to accommodate increased traffic in the area.

I didn't care about wider streets, but I did care about those trees. Not only did they provide beauty, shade and privacy, they were also a haven for tweeting birds, just feet away from my window. Within days a group of students—ecologists, anti-government activists, idealists—organized a protest. Early one chilly winter morning, a dozen or so *manifestants* climbed the trees on the opposite side of the street and, armed with blankets and mimeographed pamphlets screaming SAVE OUR TREES, settled in for a long siege. A folding table appeared on the sidewalk, manned by volunteers urging passersby to sign a petition to stop the "massacre." The ambience on Steinengraben was lively despite the cold. Jokes and snacks flew freely between the ground crew and the brave soldiers who stayed up in the trees for as long as they could bear it, replaced by others willing to show their solidarity. My task, besides shouting verbal encouragements, was to fortify the troops by handing out blankets, chocolate, rolls, hot beverages, whatever was needed to ease their discomfort. Frau Eichele, amused by our demonstration, let me borrow all her thermos bottles, which I filled with tea and coffee and brought over to the students.

Amid this hub of activity and good cheer I heard someone ask in English:

"Does anyone here speak English?"

Shoving people out of the way, I made a beeline for the stranger who had spoken.

"I do!" I shouted, waving my arm. "I do!"

The voice belonged to an American male about 5'10", Caucasian, with straight brown hair and a mustache, and wearing cool stripy pants the way only Americans can wear them and not look silly.

"Hello!"

"Hello, how are you?" I said, relishing the prospect of a full-blown conversation with a real, live American.

"Fine." He extended his hand. "I'm Allen."

"Pleased to meet you. I'm Mona."

"Mona? Like the Mona Lisa?"
I laughed.
"Exactly."
We stood there, smiling at each other.
"So, what's going on?"
"We're demonstrating to save the trees. The city is about to cut them down and we are trying to stop them. I live right over there," I added, pointing at my window across the street.

"A demonstration? That's great! I hope you can save those trees. By the way, your English is very good."

"Oh, I just love to speak English."

Allen pulled a small piece of paper from his pocket.

"Actually," he said with a sheepish look on his face, "I wonder if you could help me. I need directions."

"Of course."

"Would you happen to know where this is?"

I leaned forward, saw the address of a *Pension* in Kleinbasel.

"I'm not really sure, but I can get a map of Basel from my room."

I didn't give Allen a chance to reply.

"I won't be a minute. Just wait here."

One of the students called out from a tree. "Hey, Mona, where are you going?"

"I'll be back, don't worry."

When I returned with the map, I asked Allen if he'd had lunch yet.

"Not really . . . I wasn't . . . ."

"Do you want to get something to eat? It's freezing cold out here."

"Sure."

We walked to a small Italian restaurant where the food was good and cheap. We sat at a table covered with a red-and-white checkered cloth and ordered *spaghetti alla bolognese*. Talking to this complete stranger turned out to be the easiest thing in the world. I told him about the strained relationship I had with my parents. He listened attentively and offered advice. He described some problems he'd had with his mother in the past, which were now resolved. He was twenty-six, from Philadelphia, a college graduate with a degree in business education. Unable to find a job, he had decided to backpack his way through Europe for three months. Then he planned to go back and find a teaching position. He had been traveling since October, hitchhiking, sleeping in hostels, meeting all sorts of interesting people, and more recently staying with a friend—an American nurse named Sue—in Nuremberg. The reason for his visit to Basel was a woman, a stewardess he had met in Holland who invited him to stop by when she returned to Basel, where she lived. He had gone to her apartment the night before, hoping to spend a few days, but she had kicked him out that morning.

"Why?"

"I don't know. Changed her mind, I suppose."

"What are you going to do?"

"Go to the *Pension*, then tomorrow I'll call her up, see if we can work something out."

I did some quick thinking.

"Look, if you want, you can stay at my place." Had I gone mad? The American sitting across from me could have been an ax murderer, a rapist, an escaped prisoner. "I've got plenty of room." To make sure he understood I wasn't offering sex, I added, "You can have my bed, I'll sleep on the floor."

Allen stared at me.

"Think of the money you'll save, not having to go to that *Pension*."

"Alright," he said, after some hesitation. "Thank you very much, Mona, that's really nice of you."

"Oh, it's not a problem."

He smiled.

"You'll make a very convincing lawyer one day."

I was relieved at first, then immediately alarmed at the boldness of my gesture. But I couldn't very well renege on the offer now, could I? Why, oh why hadn't I kept my mouth shut? It was dark outside, almost six o'clock.

"What about your friends?"

"My friends?"

"Your friends in the trees."

I had run off with a foreigner and left them to fend for themselves. Clearly my commitment to the cause had its limits. Something—someone—more interesting had come along and I had split without giving my fellow demonstrators a second thought.

"They'll be fine," I said. "There were plenty of other people."

"But those were *your* trees."

I glanced at him to see if he was serious. The twinkle in his eye reassured me.

"I know, I know." But how often do you meet a total stranger with whom you instantly connect?

I gave Allen directions to the train station—he had left his backpack there, intending to do some sightseeing—and to Frau Eichele's house. As soon as I reached Steinengraben I saw the students had left. I quickly straightened out my room and went downstairs to talk to Frau Eichele. Granted, it was insane to invite a stranger into someone else's home, but then again, did she *really* have to know I had only just met Allen? I made up a story that he was an old friend who had unexpectedly arrived in Basel. Could he stay for the night? (Of course, there was always a chance that he would think twice about the offer and not show up.)

"Sure he can stay. One of the upstairs rooms is vacant. He can sleep there."

I kissed her. She was the best landlady anyone could ask for. One day I would make it up to her. As we stood in the hallway, the doorbell rang.

"That must be him," I said, my heart racing.

"Come in, come in," Frau Eichele said to Allen in halting English. "Mona has told me about you." I translated what she wanted to convey to Allen: that any friend of Mona's was welcome in her house, that he could stay in the unoccupied room on the third floor for as long as he wanted. He thanked her profusely.

"Go ahead, dear, show him the room."

For the next ten days I skipped most of my classes and took Allen sightseeing. I introduced him to my friends—Sandro invited him to view Basel from the air in his two-seater plane—dragged him to little cafés where we talked as if there was no tomorrow. I also made an appointment with a gynecologist: it was time to go on the pill.

Allen wanted to find a job at one of the U.S. military bases in Germany so that he could stay in Europe. I contemplated dropping out of law school. Frau Eichele, not anyone's fool, quickly figured out what was going on.

One evening in my room, Allen told me he loved me. I dismissed the statement with a wave of the hand.

"You don't love me."

Allen winced, looked me straight in the eye and left without a word. I sat around for a while, biting my nails, debating what to do. Finally, I went upstairs and knocked on his door.

The man of my dreams was packing his bags.

"What are you doing?" I asked in a panic.

"Packing. It's time for me to go anyway."

"But why? Why so suddenly?"

Allen stopped what he was doing and turned to face me.

"Look," he said, "I don't appreciate having my feelings shot down like that."

"I didn't believe . . . ."

"Believe it. I love you."

"But how do you know? Maybe you just think you love me. You hardly know me."

"Don't ever question my love for you!"

I was taken aback. No one had ever spoken to me about love this way.

"Okay," I whispered. Allen took me in his arms and kissed me, his body pressing hard against mine.

That was our first quarrel. We made up most eloquently, and Allen's concession was to postpone his departure by one day.

* * *

February 1, 1972

Dear Mona:

I love you!

I decided to take the train after all and I'm glad that I did. I met two very nice German ladies who tried to teach me how to correctly pronounce many different words; they were very patient with me, and as you can well imagine there was laughter everywhere. Then a group of four Yugoslavians came into our compartment and the good time that I was having became wonderful. They brought a bottle of "schnapps" with them and everyone became good friends very quickly. When I got off at Frankfurt I felt warm, happy, and a little bit dizzy.

I arrived in Nürnberg at 18:03 and when I got back to the apartment there was mail waiting for me. One of the letters was from Berlin and it read "Thanks for the application, but no dice." In other words, no possibility for me to teach in Berlin. Now for the good news. The army has another job for me, in the mornings, as a counselor. I will be told more about the job tomorrow. It pays $2.50 an hour and has the possibility of becoming a regular full-time position.

I miss you, and I love you more than I miss you, and I miss you more each day. You know that I am looking forward to seeing you in München. I am very anxious to see how the pictures came out, but I am even more anxious to see you again.

Write soon.

Can you hear my music playing
Though silent words you read?
Can you see the picture I'm painting
Through the lined white paper
Lightly clad in ink?
By the light.
Soft candle glow in the night.
You're my candle glow.
I'm the lonely night.

Fairy tales are wandering
Forgotten by the young,
Who imagine they are older,
And older they became.
By a dream.
Soft star light in the night.
You're my dream.
I'm the lonely night.
Smiling faces are hiding
Behind a crowded street.
They are lost among the neon signs
And walls that never speak.
By the light.
Soft sunrise of the night.
You're the sun.
I'm the lonely night.
I was a stranger to the light,
You were to the night.
You have filled me,
You have warmed me,
With your sweet light.
By the light.
Ever brightening the night.
You're the light.
I was the lonely night.

Love, Allen

February 11, 1972

Dear Mona:

    Ich liebe zee! Your intuitive feeling about A.P.O. is correct, for I still have not received the letter you addressed to the hospital. The area code for Nürnberg is 85.
    I read your letter over and over again, partly because I could not read your handwriting, and partly because I just felt like doing so. Please, Mona, try to write a little more clearly, because I want to read every single letter you write. There are still some words that I just, for the life of me, cannot decipher. When you write me again concerning München, tell me when and how you are coming and leaving. *Verstehen Sie?*

I have begun teaching 17 men the difficult skill of typing. I look forward to each new class. There is no doubt about it, teaching is for me, I love every minute of it.

I found out today that another position as a guidance counselor has opened up and I have been offered that job too. I guess somebody must like me, because I have only been teaching for a week now. Nobody really knows if I'm even a good teacher, let alone a good counselor.

You sound so happy and content in your letter and, of course, that makes me very, very happy. I miss you sorely. I cannot put into words my feelings now, as I write, except to say that they are all directed at you and they are truly beautiful. Schön! If you're not going to school after this month, what will you be doing? And how come you're not going?

I am very pleased that Mrs. Eichele enjoyed my letter. She was so nice to me, I will never forget her for that.

Say hello to Sandro, Sandra, Jean-Paul, Claudia, Mario, Alois, and Esther for me when you see them.

My diet consists of two cups of coffee with toast and jelly in the morning, and a bowl of rice, two slices of bread (with cheese or ham) and a couple of glasses of milk for supper at night. I have about $60.00 left and this must last me until the end of March when I will receive my paycheck.

Mona, I miss you, I do. And I want you, much more than I miss you, and I miss you sorely. Yet, with time, I have found I need you much more than I want you, and with each passing day my want grows. As great as my need may be for you, my love is greater, by far greater. And each passing day I miss you more than before. I give my love to you day after day.

No matter how the dice were tossed, it had to be—Happy together.

I love you
Allen

P.S. Send me Angelika's address in München just in case I lose the one you gave me.

Morning nestles comfortably
Between a fresh memory
And soft images unfolding.
Good day! Sunshine morning!
Fine day for a song to be sung.
Maybe a cloud or two to ride on,
Dreaming the day away.

February 12, 1972

Dear Mona:

I am assuming that you are already in München, thus this letter.

I will be teaching every afternoon this week until 17:00. At this point in time I do not know how I will get to München, only that I will get there. On Monday I will ask my class if they know of anyone who will be driving to München for the weekend. If that fails, maybe I will take the train Friday night and hitch back to Nürnberg on Monday. I'm very, very short on money and unless the ticket is reasonably priced I will have to hitch to München Saturday morning. But let us wait a few more days and perhaps a ride will appear. In any event I will write to you again on Wednesday and tell you exactly how and when I will arrive in München.

I suspected that Angelika was a very good person, because all of your friends that I met were wonderful people; no, I will go one step further, they were beautiful people. I see that Angelika too is a beautiful person. I feel happy and a bit sad at the same time. Happy, because I will be able to spend all my time with you. A bit sad because we will be doing so at the expense of Angelika. But I suppose she will be happy to see us together and in love. Tell Angelika that I thank her very much and I am, of course, looking forward to meeting her.

I want you, Mona, not to possess, rather to share experiences; thoughts; feelings. I want you, not to be mine, but to be with me, and I with you, and for us to call things "ours," not yours or mine. You make me, unknowingly perhaps, feel a rainbow of feelings and I enjoy being swept past bright reds, yellows, blues and violets with you close at my side.

My typing class is coming along very well. Each day I enjoy teaching more. I'm very happy with my position. When I see you this weekend I will tell you all about it and my future positions.

Listen! Closely! Come closer! Closer!

Allen

February 24, 1972

Dear Mona:

Arrived in Nürnberg about 12:30. My trip back was much longer than my trip down.

You and I are much closer now, in many ways, than we were before München. It seems each time we meet we discover a little bit more about each other and grow a little closer because of it. I think of you and I smile. I sense a lot of people staring at me whenever I find myself thinking of you. I want to share my warm thoughts with them, but they just walk by or lower their heads to read the printed word again, leaving me alone with you.

My class is coming along fine and I am anxious to see how my students do on their final examination, which in some way will reflect my teaching ability. I'm really more curious than concerned. It will give me a great deal of pleasure and satisfaction to see everyone do well.

I wrote a letter to Angelika to thank her. She seems like a wonderful person and I hope someday we can become good friends.

Presently I do not know for sure when I can come to Basel, only that I will come sometime between March 10 and 20. I will come!

When you write, Mona, please, take your time and write clearly. Thank you. I love you. Write soon.

Love, Allen

February 29, 1972

Dear Mona:

I love you. I have read both your letters and my feelings run parallel to yours. I miss you every day and my thoughts are about you, even when they should be somewhere else. I think about us more now than I ever did before. We have a special love, you and I, and each time we are together it gets better. I want to be with you so badly, it hurts.

I hope your cold is gone now. I knew you would get sick because of me and I feel bad about that now. But I guess you must share the bad as well as the good. It's my fault, though, that you caught the cold and I should have been strong enough to make sure you didn't catch it.

The pictures of Carnival are really great and I got a kick out of (enjoyed) looking at them. I was glad to hear that you enjoyed Carnival so much, that you forgot about your cold, at least for a little while. Tell Sandro I got his letter and will answer him.

Well, it looks like we won't be seeing each other until after the 17th but I'm happy that you got a good paying job. Mona, please write more slowly so I can understand what you're saying. I understood most of your two letters, but there are still parts of them I just can't figure out. Please, try to write a little more clearly. For me. If it isn't too much trouble. Please.

Mona, I love you. Do you know what that means? You are a part of me, of my thoughts and feelings. You are with me always. Why? Why do I love you? Is it because you are beautiful? Or because you are smart, or a good cook, or a great dresser? And

I could go on and on, listing such questions. I would answer each one with a no. I do not love you for what I can see or touch. I love you for all those things that I cannot see or touch. I love you for all those beautiful things within you, and they will remain beautiful regardless of age (yes, even when you are 65 you will be beautiful to me and I will love you deeply). What are these "things" within you that I love? Describe them? I cannot. I can only reflect them with the love that they have given me. Do you understand? My love for you was given to me by your love for me. My love for you is a reflection of what you are inside. I love you from the inside out, not the outside in. I love you, Mona, because I do.

"Thoughts After"

Dear Mona:

Is it strange of me to think? Is it just a dream of mine? You called me. I love you. Circles in my ears. Noises in my eyes. I ache for you. Thoughts captured in my heart. Unspoken words to you. Trying to be smart. My love humbled me. I spoke not what I meant. I meant not what I spoke. A confused child was I. Is this what love can do? Can you forgive my incompetence on the phone? I was swelled with feeling. I love you. I love you more than you know. I know. I love you more than you realize. Can you trust my love? Of that I can never convince you in words. I can only love you. What am I saying? I know not. I am writing my feelings, as they come . . . one by one. I trust my feelings as I do your love. Am I a fool? Perhaps. But I am unconcerned. You are my concern. You are my love. It is your love that I need. I need you. I confess. I do.

I'm coming. I will see if I can get off a few days. I want to be with you longer than a day, or two, or even a week. Do I sound like a child? Foolish? At this moment, right now, I am a child. Helpless. Helpless to touch you, speak with you, save this letter. Helpless to stop dreaming of the weekend when I come to Basel, as a child dreams of Christmas. Foolish boy! Are you thinking that now? I hope you aren't.

I love you and miss you
Allen

P.S. I will write again. That's not a threat . . . it's a promise.

Tell me that you love me.
Not because you have to.
Not because you want to.
Not because, because at all.
But merely that you do.

March 4, 1972

Dear Mona:

After reading your letter, and I think I understand the questions or problems it conveyed, I felt that I should be with you. Instead I'm writing my thoughts hoping that they will provide some answers, or at least give you a different perspective. Keep in mind, though, that although I love you and want only the best for you, this does not mean that my ideas are correct. Nevertheless, I present them hoping that I can be of some help. I love you, Mona.

Your parents love you. The idea of the "contract" was created out of their love and concern for you. They want the best for you and evidently felt that the "contract" would be a stabilizing influence on you, that it would help you to mature. They felt, or at least your mother felt, that the "contract" would influence you in a positive manner, and in the long run, make you a better person because of it.

Your father, from what he wrote you in his letter, has his doubts, it seems, about the "contract" and his overall posture concerning you. Your mother, on the other hand, evidently felt and feels she knows you better than your father, or even yourself. Now, however, your father seems to be questioning your mother's action, at least concerning the "contract," and perhaps your mother's past as well as present thoughts and attitudes towards you. In other words, your father is saying: Was I wrong? Was my wife wrong? He's not quite sure, but the question is in his mind and he seems to be troubled with the doubt it now arouses.

Parents are not infallible; they make mistakes too, generally out of their love for their child. It is difficult to admit to one's own errors, without the help of a second person (usually a friend, but not always). It is far more difficult for parents to admit that they made a mistake in raising their child and almost impossible for them to do so of their own volition.

Parents are cast into a very difficult role: the complete and utter responsibility of developing another human being. If their child seems (to them) to be developing in a manner that is unacceptable, they as parents are compelled, out of their love and concern, to alter that development. They do so for the best interest of the child. After all, they are the parents and as such know (or think they know) what is good or detrimental for their child. Therefore any action taken must be for the betterment of the child (or so the parents conclude). This casts the child into, perhaps, a far more difficult role: that of determining for himself (or herself) when he is capable of his own decisions and actions concerning present and future development. Thus you have the potential for misunderstanding between parent and child.

Children, of course, love their parents, if for nothing else, out of sheer gratitude for the warmth, comfort and security they provide or provided. Hence, it is difficult for children to disagree with their parents, particularly on their own development, without feeling some degree of guilt (generally a feeling of betrayal). Guilt is an extremely difficult emotion to deal with on any level, but especially so when it is felt by a child towards his parents. The parents can complicate or compound the child's struggle for self-determination and identification out of their love, doing more harm than good.

There comes a point, in a child-parent relationship, when the parents must assume a passive role in their child's development, transferring the bulk of the responsibility to the child. When this occurs depends to a great extent on the parents' realization that their child has matured and grown (for better or for worse) sufficiently to handle and cope with life. For example, a bird can care for its young and do all that is possible to prepare her offspring for flight (the culmination of the hen's responsibility to her offspring), but there comes a point when the offspring must fly by itself. The hen cannot fly for her offspring. Likewise, parents cannot live their child's life. The sooner the parents and child realize this will determine the ease with which they will undergo this important transition of the child's development and child-parent relationship.

Your father seems to have realized at least some of what I have been writing. Your mother, evidently, still looks upon you as an adolescent, incapable of facing life without her support. You seem to be confused about your whole relationship with your parents. If you feel that in some way you have betrayed their trust and love (and I suspect you do), you must ask yourself why? It seems to me, however, that if anyone should feel guilty about betraying trust and love it should be your parents. What is it they want from you? Have you ever asked them, especially your mother? What exactly does your mother expect you to be or do in life? Continually repent for something you did, or were supposed to have done, as an adolescent?! You owe your mother and father nothing! It is they who owe you everything! Mona, listen very carefully to what I have to say. You are no longer an adolescent; you are a woman now, an adult, just as much as your mother and father. The only difference between you, or me, and your parents is that we are establishing our lives as adults. We are making our future. We are learning about life and experiencing life, much like our parents have. Your parents and my parents are more experienced in life, for the simple reason that they have lived it longer. We can benefit from their experience and they can help us, when we seek their help. But we cannot expect, nor can our parents expect us to live our lives as they think best. It is we who have the responsibility of our actions, of our life, of our future, not our parents! They have prepared us for life the best way they knew (not necessarily the best way possible). For that we can thank them without forever remaining their humble and grateful servants.

Mona, you and I are adults. To be an adult does not necessarily mean that we are not going to make mistakes in life; quite to the contrary, we will make many. But what is an adult? It is when the bulk, if not all of the decision-making responsibility of your life is made by you. Even though your parents are supplying you with funds, it is you who are making the decisions on a day-to-day basis. Maturity is another question. One can be an adult, but an immature adult. I hope you're following me. Maturity depends on how you use your decision-making ability as an adult. Maturity is when you have enough sense to make a decision for yourself that you may not like but is necessary for your own well-being. Some adults never really mature and I am sure you have met a few. Maturity is something that each of us must find in our own way. We cannot turn to our parents for help in this matter because they are too subjective. In our parents' eyes we will, perhaps, never be mature, even if they recognize us to be adults. Why? Because we have become a very sensitive and intricate part of our parents' total being. It hurts them to lose us. They know from the day we are born that the day will come when we will leave them. Because of their love for us, they can sometimes hinder our growing up.

Mona, Mona, Mona, am I being a help? I want to help you, but I do not want my love to blind me and hurt you in the process. Have I written too much? Or too little? The only thing I'm sure of is our love.

You told me in a previous letter that you have a job and that I shouldn't come to Basel until after the 17th of March. I will probably come either on the 17th or the following weekend, the 24th. When I come I will try to get four days off but that depends on my boss. In any case I will come for at least Friday night, Saturday, and Sunday.

Your poem was really, really good. In fact, it was beautiful. I wish I could write that way.

I'm still looking for an apartment and I think I may have one within the next week. I hope!

Mona, I love you. Whenever you feel troubled just remember that I love you, that I care. It's not easy now because we are so far apart. But we are only separated by a physical barrier, that of distance. Our love transcends the physical world, it can move across valleys or the highest mountains. My love is with you always, no matter where you are.

Instead of biting your nails, think of me. Think of us together.

I love you more than life itself.

Allen

March 13, 1972

My dear Mona:

For some reason I have the unshakeable feeling that you are angry or upset with me. I hope I'm wrong. It's just a feeling that I have.

To travel from Nürnberg to Basel round-trip costs 90 Marks. I don't even have 90 Marks; so the train is out. It takes about 6 1/2 hours by train to get to Basel, so I figure if I hitch it will take me about 8 hours. I will try to get two days off, besides the weekend. That will allow us at least two whole days together. No matter what, though, I will be in Basel Friday night, or early Saturday morning (2am). I will see about getting a ride with someone, but I doubt if I will. In any case I will be in Basel this weekend. Do you understand? I'm coming to Basel because I want to see you very much. If you don't want to see me, tell me.

Today I start working full-time as a counselor.

Still haven't found an apartment, but I'm looking very hard. Still waiting for my paycheck.

Mona, I hope you understand, really understand, my present position. I'm living, right now, on the charity of some good friends. I'm trying to get on my feet financially. As soon as I get paid and settled here in Nürnberg, we will be able to see each other more often. I wish I could be speaking to you in person now. Well, in any case, I will see you this weekend.

> Do you doubt the light of the morning sun?
> Do you doubt the rise or ebb of the ocean's tide?
> Do you doubt the floral rainbow of spring's mantel?
> Then, my love, you can never doubt.
> My love burns, as a morning sun never sets.
> My love throbs, with the consistency of the ocean's tide.
> My love shines, with the color of spring's bright mantel.
> If I were to claim that my love
> Could not get any higher
> Then, my love, I would be a liar.

Your admirer, adorer, wooer, beau, sweetheart, swain, young man and flame who likes, fancies, cares for, takes an interest in, sympathizes with, is in love with, regards, reveres, takes to, sets his affections on, idolizes, makes much of, holds dear, prizes, hugs, and cherishes you.

Allen

March 22, 1972

Dear Mona:

Your handwriting remains the same: confusing, yet lovable.

My little speech turned out to be a success and I was well received by the battalion commanders and the post commander. I will be interviewed tomorrow by AFN (American Forces Network) about Project Transition and it will be broadcast sometime next week. (I will write to tell you the date and time as soon as I find out.)

I really didn't want to be interviewed because I do not feel, at this point in time, that I have enough information or knowledge about Project Transition. But other people seem to think I do, so I accepted.

On Monday I met with a Major from the 123rd S+T (Supply + Transport) Battalion First Armored Division and we agreed to begin planning a training program in auto mechanics for soldiers who have six months or less of active duty. Now I have in the planning stages a training program with a Warrant Officer of ADP (Advanced Data Processing) as well as the Major. I'm very enthusiastic about my work and enjoying it more and more each day.

I saw the landlady today and I am to meet with her again this Saturday, so hopefully I will find out exactly what apartment I/we are to live in and when I/we can move in. I have not yet told her about you and do not intend to until I have paid her and have moved in. Don't worry, though, we will have a place of our own in April.

It pleases me that you sought the advice of Claudia, Sandra, and Mrs. Eichele and that they encouraged you to break that ridiculous contract and the unhealthy relationship you presently have with your parents.

You're growing up, Mona, and I suspect that within a few short years you will be a lady, not a woman, but a real lady. Do you understand? You have many fine qualities, Mona, behind that nail-bitten façade. I saw them from the very first and they show more and more with each passing meeting. You will outclass me someday once you get it all together and then, perhaps . . . but that's a bit of a ways off in the future.

I believe you when you write or say "I love you" because I trust you, your words and actions.

Mona, I love you but I will not let my love suffocate you. So that you do not misunderstand what I have just written, I will explain it a bit more. Love is such a strong emotion that it can sometimes destroy or harm the person to whom it is directed. One can have such a great love, and I confess that I do towards you, that unintentionally he can possess or envelop the one he loves to such an extent, to the point of suffocation or emasculation, that his love will be more detrimental than helpful. In other words, when you come to Nürnberg you will be met with a love that wants you, and I want you, Mona, but that will never demand or force you to any decision. My love for you will help you but never will it expect you to abide by it. I am with you, for you and I will be with you in April and wanting the best for you. I trust you, and in you. I recognize that you are you, and so my love for you will be shared with you, not forced upon you. Do you understand my love for you? It is incomplete, it is nothing without you. I love you. I want you. I need you.

Love, Allen

March 26, 1972

Dear Mona:

This past week I have been very busy meeting various commanders and counseling soldiers. It's a lot of work but I really enjoy it and I am quite happy with my position at the present time.

Still haven't spoken to the landlady, but I know I will see her this week because she has to come around to collect the rent. Please be patient. I will have an apartment.

Tomorrow I speak again to all the Battalion commanders. I have done a lot to get the ball rolling for Project Transition. Now I must be careful that the momentum that I have built does not slow down.

That's about all for now.

Your eyes closed,
Feel as I touch you,
Warmly within your mind's eye.

Closer, I whisper,
Snugly within your ear,
As I draw your heart close to mine.

Have I ever left you?
Never.
You only have to look within.
Love.
My love you'll always find.

Softly speak the words we're meant for.
Slowly the echo grows . . .
I love you.
I love you with all my heart.

At 15:00 think of what I have written and I will be thinking of you each day especially at that hour. I'm giving you my phone number. I would want to call you, but I just don't have the money. If it is too expensive to call, don't.

Give my love to everyone.

Love, Allen

LEAVING EUROPE

Tuesday

Dear Mona:

  Just received your letter today. I miss you very much. I feel lonely without you.
  The landlady was here Saturday but I missed her. I found out today, however, that I will be moving into an apartment this Saturday, Sunday, or Monday. The landlady left a message for me with a couple who have been living here for quite some time (about 5 years, you will meet them when you come) that I definitely have an apartment. As soon as I actually, physically move in I will write to you. Bring your wedding ring with you, for I have decided to tell the landlady that we were married in Switzerland (I think that would eliminate any possible problems that might occur with her). As things stand now you will be able to come to Nürnberg next week. I am getting very impatient to move into the apartment and if I don't move in this weekend I will look elsewhere, but again, I feel confident that I will be moving in this weekend.
  My job is becoming more of a joy with each passing day. Much has been happening and I'm beginning to accomplish some of the goals I have set for the program.
  Next time we are together we can stay together for as long as you wish to. As for me, I want to learn more of life with you, to grow old with you, to be together. Until death do us part.

Love, Allen

Chapter Four: GERMANY

I arrived in Nuremberg, without warning, that Saturday afternoon. Marcus, a student I barely knew, had volunteered to drive all my worldly possessions in his overheating 2CV, just for the pleasure of my company.

Bärenschanzstrasse 51, a building populated solely with Americans, for the most part young servicemen and their families, stood in front of us. I prayed that Allen would be there, either at Sue's apartment or, preferably, in his own quarters. Marcus and I stepped through the archway leading to a small courtyard and the stairs. Allen had told me that Sue lived on the second floor. Filled with anticipation, I rang her doorbell. No answer. I tried again. A soldier in uniform walked past us in the hallway. I asked him if by any chance he knew Allen.

"Allen? I think he's one floor up."

I wanted to race upstairs but, for Marcus' sake, controlled myself. On the third floor, a door was open. I peered in.

"Hello?"

"Mona! What . . . what are you doing here?" Allen dropped the broom and dustpan he was holding and rushed towards me. We embraced.

"Allen, this is Marcus."

"Hello, Marcus," Allen said, shaking his hand.

"Marcus drove me all the way here," I explained. "Wasn't that nice of him?"

"Very nice. Thank you, Marcus."

He turned to look at me and laughed. "You couldn't wait any longer, could you?"

"In your letters you kept saying, 'I'm going to have an apartment next week, I promise, *next* week, and if not, then the following week . . . .' So I decided to come."

"And what if I didn't get the apartment? I literally got the keys an hour ago."

I smiled. "I knew you would."

Allen offered to take Marcus for a drink at the corner *Gasthaus*, but eager to get back on the road, he declined. We unloaded the car and carried my belongings to the third floor.

At the curb Allen and I said goodbye to Marcus and watched the Citroën disappear around the corner.

"Well, Mona," Allen said, "you are full of surprises, aren't you?" He took my hand and gazed at me. "I can't believe you're here."

The efficiency Allen had moved into was tiny. Although it had a separate kitchen, bathroom, and living room with a pullout couch, space was so limited that two people couldn't stand in the kitchen at the same time. Ditto for the pint-sized bathroom. The flat came with bulky furniture that had seen better days. When, out of curiosity, I whacked the sofa bed to test its firmness, a cloud of dust flew out; I did it again, for fun, and more particles rose and filled the room. Allen had taken great pains to sweep the floor, wipe the table, scrub the kitchen sink. Next he was going to attack the bathroom. Nothing, not the sagging, mildewed shower curtain, nor the dirty, rusty hotplate could dampen my enthusiasm.

To Allen and me, this space represented heaven, simply because it was ours.

On Monday morning Allen went to work and I went looking for a job. Life as a couple—pooling our resources, shouldering responsibilities together—had begun. Now it was Allen's turn to introduce me to his friends: Sue, generous to a fault; Margie and her husband Tony, former opera singers; Bob, a dashing Army captain; Rod, a retired Army sergeant working as a freelance photographer, and his second wife Red, a tall, buxom redhead with an appetite for life. Allen had spoken to everyone about my impending arrival and I was welcomed like a bride. Even the landlady, dismissed by all the tenants as a mean old bat interested only in collecting greenbacks, was pleasant to me. For one thing I was Swiss, and she loved Switzerland ("so clean, so beautiful"), for another I was able to communicate with her in German. Allen had insisted, as a precaution, that we tell her we were married. He didn't want to risk getting evicted for living with his girlfriend. The landlady had already questioned him about his arrangement with Sue, which, he had assured her, was only temporary. While in Munich he and I had bought the cheapest fake wedding rings we could find in a department store. Every few weeks we replaced them because the rings would turn green over time. It was all part of the fun of pretending to be married.

Papa, meanwhile, took a different view. An envelope addressed to me came in the mail one day. Inside I found a sheet torn from his prescription pad with the words: *I hope you know about contraception.* It was signed, Your father.

I wept and kicked the air and wept some more. Read and reread the single sentence. How, I wanted to know, can parents be so cruel to their own children? Allen held me, listened, explained it all to me.

On the job front things were looking up. Thanks to Allen's connections, I was hired as a secretary for someone he knew at the main Army base in Nuremberg. Mr. Davis and I got along famously. Laid-back, with a quick wit, he went out of his way to be helpful. Since I was a Third National (neither American nor German), paperwork had to be put though the proper channels to enable me to work there. Mr. Davis took care of it all.

Allen, though American, was a local hire and as such did not have access to the PX, or Post Exchange, where U.S. military personnel could buy American goods at very low prices. He relied on the kindness of friends to supply us with a few staples, my first exposure to American food. Money was tight. Allen worked at Merrell Barracks in Fürth, where twice a month we brought our laundry bags to a Laundromat catering to American servicemen. We could use U.S. currency there, and it was much cheaper than going to a local facility. Doing the laundry turned into quite an expedition. On the appointed day, right after work, we would each lug a tightly packed laundry bag to the nearest streetcar stop. In Fürth we took another *Strassenbahn* and walked several blocks to the Laundromat, which was always crowded. We would brace ourselves for two or three hours of washing, drying, folding, and stuffing our clean clothes back into the laundry bags. At last we retraced our steps, hoping it wouldn't rain. Dinner on those nights consisted mainly of chocolate bars and potato chips wolfed down in the streetcar, to the other passengers' evident displeasure.

My memory of those days is one of contrasts: on one hand, the passion of first love, on the other, the drabness of the Germans around us. Many wore dark green coats and we had to endure disapproving looks for wearing somewhat more colorful outfits. Then there was the pushing. Pushing to get on the *Strassenbahn,* pushing in the elevator, pushing at the butcher's.

When we could afford it, Allen and I liked to buy sausages at the local butcher's. One day, as I was waiting in line to be served, an old woman pushed past me and tried to order ahead of me. Unfortunately for her, that was the day I decided I had been pushed one time too many.

"Oh no, you don't!" I shouted in English.

The woman muttered something about not speaking English. I grabbed her elbow and pointed at the spot behind me.

"You understand perfectly well what I'm saying." From the corner of my eye I could see Allen gingerly retreating towards the door. "You wait your turn, like everybody else."

By now the small shop was abuzz with commentary from the other housewives, mostly older women. The pushy one, who appeared cowed, stayed put. I ordered my sausages and left, glaring at her on the way out.

"Serves her right," I told Allen outside.

"Why didn't you speak to her in German?" he asked, amused.

"I don't know. It just came out in English. It's such a great language to be mad in."

Allen and I settled into our little routine, going to work, enjoying simple pleasures such as sightseeing in the *Altstadt*, socializing with our American friends, occasionally treating ourselves to a hearty meal of *Leberkäse* and warm potato salad at the corner *Gasthaus*, or roasted chicken at the Wienerwald restaurant chain. At home, I was learning how to cook. One evening I tried a recipe from the cookbook Charlotte had given me as a parting gift. *English Cooking*, it was called. For some reason, I chose to make kedgeree, a mixture of smoked fish, rice, and hard-boiled eggs. I anxiously waited for Allen to put a forkful in his mouth.

"Very nice," he said.

I burst into tears. I knew it was inedible and here he was, lying to spare my feelings.

On a wide, straight stretch of road between Nuremberg and Fürth, at Number 110 Fürther Strasse, stood the massive, austere *Landgericht* (regional court) where Nazi war criminals were tried after World War II. Whenever we walked past the courthouse, which wasn't far from our apartment, Allen would remark that, as a Jew, the mere sight of that building sent chills up his spine. Other reminders of the Nazi presence in town were the former Nazi Party rally grounds at Zeppelinwiese. Allen and I once visited the stands where people hailed the Führer—we shivered both from the cold dampness of the place and its historic implications. But there were other sights in Nuremberg: the quaint little streets leading up to the Kaiserburg, the half-timbered houses at Tiergärtnertor, the *Schöner Brunnen* on Hauptmarkt. On Saturday mornings Allen and I did our weekly shopping, fighting our way through the swarms of people crowding the supermarkets and department stores before early closing time. You could forget about shopping on Sundays: everything, except the odd *Bäkerei* or *Konditorei*, was closed.

In the fall Mr. Davis offered me a new position. Due to lack of funds, the MOS (Military Occupational Specialty) Library had fallen into disrepair. It needed a complete revamping. Would I be interested? I hesitated because I lacked training as a librarian. Allen encouraged me to accept, pointing out that it would be more challenging than my present position, and pay more money, which we could certainly use. I was shown into a dusty room littered with books, falling shelves, and plenty of cobwebs. Working alone, I cleaned up the bookcases, moved boxes, sifted through piles of manuals, sorting them by topic and call numbers, until the space looked like a library again. Librarian by default, I was pleased when military personnel started coming in to admire the transformation and borrow books.

Over the next few months Allen and I were able to save enough money to buy a used Volkswagen. We still did our laundry at the American Laundromat, but at least now we could drive there. On Sundays we explored the German countryside, taking in the sights like proper tourists: Rothenburg ob der Tauber, Bamberg, Ansbach, Munich—where Angelika had gotten married, without fuss, to a fellow law student. We traveled to Salzburg for a short holiday, staying at a modest *Pension*. The door to our room had a glass panel that looked on to a circular hallway. All night long we heard people in varying stages of inebriation go up and down the stairs, passing within inches of the small bed where we lay, huddled under the covers, unable to sleep. During the Christmas season, we discovered the *Christkindlmarkt,* with its festive stalls selling old-fashioned wooden toys, glittering tree ornaments, *Lebkuchen* (gingerbread) and glasses of *Glühwein* (warm mulled wine). The cold weather and early nightfall went unnoticed as we strolled among the decorated firs and handcrafted scenes of Nativity, listening to Advent music. Caught in the spirit of the moment, Germans at their most cheerful and tourists mingled happily. Children of all ages, their eyes wide in wonderment, were on their best behavior.

Things were going so well that we considered moving out of our "American ghetto." Allen and I saw an apartment in Erlangen, a pleasant university town where we often went to escape from dull, dreary Fürth. We liked Erlangen with its less conformist population, lovely English gardens, quirky *Hugenottenbrunnen,* and the little café that served hot chocolate with mounds of whipped cream. The apartment was stunning. We got a glimpse of what life could be. And then Allen received a call. The American High School in Ludwigsburg had a sudden opening for a typing teacher, starting in February. This was a great opportunity for Allen to finally do what he was trained to do: teach business subjects to high school students. Maybe, if all went well, the school would offer him a permanent position for the following school year. To work for the Department of Defense Dependent Schools (DODDS, or DOD for short) was Allen's dream.

We started packing.

Ludwigsburg, in Baden-Württemberg, lies just north of Stuttgart, a city with a very different feel from Nuremberg. As Nuremberg spelled conservative, xenophobic, and oppressively past-oriented, Stuttgart conjured up openness, a distinct cosmopolitan flavor, modern art. We searched in vain for affordable housing in Ludwigsburg, and after scouring the countryside, ended up in a hamlet called Grossingersheim, where we rented a furnished apartment in the basement of a private house attached to a beverage distribution business. The friendly owner and his family lived upstairs with their gorgeous boxer. Allen and I were thrilled with our new digs: clean, with a fully fitted kitchen, and plenty of space to move around. I quickly found a job as a phone operator at Gelbe Seiten, the German Yellow Pages, in Stuttgart. Allen drove me to work in the morning and picked me up at five, routinely passing by the enormous *Residenzschloss*, a masterpiece of Baroque architecture, on the way home. Living in castle-crazy Germany can, in due time, make you complacent about the grandeur of your surroundings.

Allen had begun to talk about marriage, a topic that did not go over well with me. I wanted to continue living with him, unfettered by the conventions of marriage. In fact, it annoyed me so much to have to wear a plastic "wedding" ring that I threatened more than once to throw it to the wind. Allen was a patient man. He tried to convince me that being married would make things easier for us in case his short-term contract was not renewed and he had to go back to the States. "I'll join you on a visitor's visa," I insisted, "no problem." He suggested we go to the American Consulate in Frankfurt to get up-to-date information. I resisted, and let out a choice oath as he left the room. I saw him getting into the car. I opened our bedroom window and shouted after him. He ignored me. Pissed, I took off the ring and threw it into the flowerbeds.

The only other row I'd had with Allen since we moved in together took place in Nuremberg, when I berated him for cozying up to a pretty girl, a friend of Sue's. He assured me that there was no reason whatsoever for me to be jealous. I remained unconvinced and called him a bastard. Allen rarely lost his temper, but on that occasion he pinned me against the wall and roared:

"Never, you hear, *never* call me that again!"

I mumbled some excuse about English not being my mother tongue, and he let go of me.

Around that time I received an envelope addressed to me at my parents' home in Switzerland. Maman, with whom I kept in touch despite the cooling of our relationship, had crossed out the Berne address and replaced it with the current one. The sender's name was clearly written on the back of the envelope. The fact that my mother chose to forward it to me—rather than, say, dispose of it with no one ever being the wiser for it—was surprising. Yet a greater surprise lay inside: François reminisced about the past and wanted to see me again. I held on to the letter for months. But I never replied.

My parents were in nearby Tübingen for a conference. I saw this as a chance to try to reconnect with Papa. Trembling, I dialed the number Maman had given me and asked to speak to my father. They had to page him. The wait was almost unbearable.

"*Allô?*" a gruff voice said finally.
"Dad? It's me." Deep breath. "Your daughter!"
Silence.
"What daughter? I no longer have a daughter."
Click.

Maman decided it was time to meet Allen. One morning she took the train from Tübingen and the three of us met at the Stuttgart train station. I hadn't seen her in almost a year and waved as soon as I caught sight of her fur coat. She didn't respond. *My own mother doesn't even recognize me,* I thought bitterly. Then I remembered that I had recently cut my hair very short. We found each other, kissed, and I introduced Allen. For a while we all sat on a bench in the station. Maman spoke mostly with Allen, and he smiled his kind smile at her, nodding, agreeing. Complaining that she was feeling a draft, my mother led us to a café near the *Hauptbahnhof* where we ordered tea and coffee.

While I nibbled on a roll, Maman tried to justify her position of neutrality in the dispute between her husband and her daughter.

"You cannot be neutral when it comes to your children," Allen told her.

Maman continued to press her point.

"I understand," he said, "but I do not agree."

My mother stared at Allen in astonishment.

"You do not agree?"

He smiled.

"That's right, I do not agree. I understand your position, but I do not agree with it."

Maman seemed puzzled, perhaps by the fact that someone could disagree with her so calmly. Years later, she still referred to that conversation. It made her instantly respect Allen, which was good news for me.

Shortly after that episode Allen and I drove to Basel to see old friends and celebrate *Fasnacht*. The Basel Carnival, which starts on the Monday before Lent and lasts three days, is eerily enchanting: at 4 a.m. the whole city turns off its lights, and adults as well as children, some carrying flashlights, descend upon it to watch troupes of masqueraders—or cliques, as they are known—march and play fifes and drums. Each clique, wearing elaborate costumes and masks, selects a specific theme to comment on, which is displayed on a large, cloth-covered lantern of original design. The narrow medieval streets are filled with music and pageantry, good humor and political satire—the latter especially appreciated by the locals, as it is all in *Basudütsch*. To warm themselves, participants stop at restaurants offering traditional dishes of onion pie and flour soup. For those three days, the people of Basel lead joyful lives. Work becomes secondary, rules are flung aside, all talk revolves around Carnival. Then everything goes back to normal, until the following year.

We went to say hello to Frau Eichele, who welcomed us with open arms and let us stay in Allen's old room. Sandra and Jean-Paul treated us to a Brazilian feast, during which Sandro, in his habitual role as court jester, provided ongoing entertainment.

Before heading back to Baden-Württemberg, we decided to make a detour through Paris. Allen had never been there, and I was dying to show him around. What began as a perfectly romantic interlude ended in Kafkaesque drama. I lost my passport at the Louvre. Before leaving the museum, I looked through my purse to make sure I had everything and, lo and behold, the red passport was gone. Panic gripped me, then the floodgates opened. We stepped outside as Allen tried to think clearly. "We'll go to the Swiss Embassy," he said, "they'll give you temporary papers, and when we get back you can apply for a new passport." It was a good plan. We found the embassy—it was almost closing time. I spoke to someone about my predicament, certain that help was on the way, and that this little slice of Switzerland in the midst of Paris would prove to be our salvation. Strangely, my request for some sort of identification was met with stony indifference.

"How do we know that you really are who you say you are?"

"Call my parents in Berne. They'll vouch for me."

My father was, at the time, director of the Maison Suisse, an organization for Swiss students at the University of Paris. I begged the person to *please* call that number—surely people at the Maison Suisse would confirm that they knew my father. By now, several employees had gathered to see what the commotion was about. There were officials on the steps, looking down at me without an ounce of sympathy. Seeing that my pleas were falling on deaf ears, I threw a fit.

"What's the purpose of having an embassy, then? I'm a Swiss citizen and I just lost my passport. For heaven's sake, do something! Give me a piece of paper so at least I can cross the border without being arrested!"

The embassy closed its doors on us. We found ourselves on the sidewalk, walking aimlessly. "You should report the loss to the police," we had been advised. That took hours. At last we sat down in a café and took stock of the situation. There was no point in staying in loathsome Paris. But without a passport, how would I be able to cross into Germany? We had to get into Switzerland first.

We traced the exact route we would take, the idea being to cross at a very small border post in the Jura late that night. If we were lucky, the border patrol wouldn't ask for our papers.

When we pulled up at the *douane* in the early morning hours, the French guard looked half asleep. On the Swiss side, one lone uniformed guard was talking to people in the car ahead of us, a car with Swiss license plates. Allen and I had plates that immediately identified us as Americans connected to U.S. military installations in Germany. The guard, leaning into the passenger side window, kept on chatting and laughing, and didn't pay us any attention. We sat still, not saying a word. Finally, he glanced our way and waved us through with impatience. We waited until we cleared the corner and let out a scream.

"We made it! We are in Switzerland!"

Sandra and Jean-Paul had been notified of our possible arrival. They offered to put us up for the night, no matter how late we got to Basel, which was very late.

Having started out as a *Telefonistin* at Gelbe Seiten, I was asked if I wanted to do some proofreading. Sure, I said, even though proofreading line after tiny line in a phone book was not my idea of fun. But it was a job, which paid part of the rent, and my bosses loved me. So much so that they were willing to give me official working papers and the opportunity to become a translator, if I committed to remain there.

Meanwhile, it had become apparent that Allen wasn't going to be hired as a permanent teacher at Ludwigsburg American High School. To do so he would have to apply to DOD in the States and then, as long as he was accepted and there was an opening, he could be transferred to one of their schools anywhere in the world.

We did have to address the issue of what to do come summer.

Our visit to the American Consulate in Frankfurt to inquire about visas was disheartening. If I planned to accompany Allen to the States as a Swiss citizen, I needed a tourist visa, which would be valid for three months only; in addition, someone in the States had to sponsor me. "But I don't know anyone in the States," I lamented. Allen wrote to his parents to ask them if they would sponsor me. They agreed.

Allen knew me well by then, far better than I knew myself. He let me arrive at *his* conclusion—that we should get married before going to the States—in my own time, on what I believed to be my own terms.

In June we packed our belongings and returned to Nuremberg, or more precisely Fürth, where Rod and Red lived. The plan was for us to get married there and fly out to Philadelphia in August.

Rod and Red let us stay in their guestroom. We spent hours filling out forms to satisfy the requirements of the bureaucracies involved—an American civilian marrying a Swiss citizen on German soil did present some challenges. The date was set for August 3rd. Because Allen didn't understand German, an interpreter had to be secured for the civil ceremony at the Fürth City Hall.

"They just want to make sure you know what you're getting into," Rod teased Allen.

We had our witnesses lined up: Rod, Red, Sue, and Sandro, who would drive up from Basel with his new movie camera.

Rod and Red were thoughtful hosts. Food, drinks, massages, the use of their Westfalia camper (since we had already sold our car), you name it: all was tendered with no expectation of anything in return. And we had nothing to offer in return, except the picture of young love. Rod and Red were an interesting couple, unconventional, uninhibited (if their loud and frequent lovemaking was any indication), secure in their relationship, both having endured disastrous first marriages.

On the eve of our wedding day, Allen got drunk.

I had never seen him drunk before and was disgusted. He threw up all over the living room floor. I refused to clean up the mess. Instead, I withdrew to the guestroom to reflect on the wisdom of marrying such a man.

Early next morning Allen was back to his cheerful, normal self. He showered, put on a clean pair of pants and a short-sleeved shirt. My outfit consisted of jeans, a red, Indian cotton blouse interwoven with gold threads—to which Allen fastened the white corsage Rod had given him—and leather sandals. The wedding was scheduled for 7 am. Rod, Red, Allen and I climbed into the camper, followed by Sandro and Sue in their respective cars, and made our way to the *Rathaus*—with my future husband commenting on the odds of getting married in a "rat-house."

The judge, a giant of a man, greeted us formally, his grip crushing our hands. Next to him stood the interpreter. The third official, a very short man in comic contrast to the judge's stature, introduced himself as the court clerk. All witnesses took up their positions (I never saw Rod and Red looking so solemn). The ceremony took twenty minutes at the most. When it was time to sign the register, I mistakenly signed my maiden name. The clerk raised his arms in distress.

"*Nein! Nein!*" he exclaimed, "you must sign your married name!"

Everyone laughed. We were officially married. Sandro, self-appointed recorder of the event, bounced around the room to get the best shots.

When we stepped outside, it was raining. Rod, Red and Sue excused themselves; they had to go to work. Allen complained of feeling under the weather. I offered to stay home with him. He declined, explained that he just needed to sleep off the previous night's excesses.

"Go have fun with Sandro!" he urged.

After we dropped him off, Sandro and I spent the rest of the day sightseeing. We drove to the center of Nuremberg and walked around the Old Town, playfully jostling each other under the small umbrella; we stopped for cake in a *Konditorei*, devoured sausages on the street. Every so often we would commiserate on Allen's fate on his special day. But wasn't it Allen himself who had encouraged us to have a good time?

When, a few days later, I asked my husband why he had gotten drunk the day before our wedding, he replied, "I guess I was a little scared."

Shortly after the wedding we went touring with Rod and Red and wound up in southern Bavaria, a landscape dotted with onion domes, the ripe smell of cow manure, wild flowers overrunning meadows, snow-capped peaks looming in the distance. At Chiemsee we admired the lake and took a boat to Herreninsel where majestic Herrenchiemsee Castle—yet another of Mad King Ludwig's designs—lies. We drove up to Berchtesgaden, though I didn't particularly want to see Hitler's alpine redoubt in Obersalzberg. We shared hearty meals, and while Rod, Red and Allen enjoyed local beer—I'd rather die of thirst than drink the stuff—in traditional *Biergärten,* I sipped cider and soaked up the fresh mountain air.

So much for our little farewell-to-Europe trip. A few days before we were scheduled to fly out, a registered letter came for Allen. It was an offer to teach at Brussels American School. Without a moment's hesitation, Allen signed the contract and we left for Belgium.

Chapter Five: BELGIUM

At the Gare Centrale in Brussels we were met by a married couple, both teachers at BAS, who had volunteered to show us around for the weekend. Drop-dead gorgeous *and* smart, they evidently reflected the caliber of the faculty at Brussels American School. It was exhilarating to be immersed in francophone culture for a change. I drooled over the elegant boulevards lined with famed *chocolatiers,* quirky Art Nouveau houses, bohemian hangouts, splendid restaurants.

Allen and I had chosen a small, modest hotel in Sterrebeek, not far from the school, as our base to look for lodgings. Classes were about to start, so we didn't have much time. We searched in Kraainem, Woluwe-St-Lambert and Woluwe-St-Pierre until our feet ached, and finally found an apartment we could afford in Stockel, at Val des Seigneurs. The landlords, a charming elderly couple living on Avenue Baron Albert d'Huart, seemed delighted to rent to us.

The nicely furnished studio had a balcony running along its entire width, with large bay windows letting in all the light. We were now part of a community of worldly residents, people who enjoyed delicacies of all sorts, people with an unmistakable *joie de vivre.*

I had thought initially that I might get a job, but discovered that holding a Swiss passport in Brussels was a hindrance, not an asset. Common Market nationals had clear priority; even American citizens—a group to which, despite my marriage to Allen, I didn't belong—had a better chance of finding employment than non-EEC members. The only offer I got, editorial work for a shady publication housed in the basement of a building downtown, would have meant getting paid under the table, and I didn't think that was a good idea. So off I went exploring every day, taking the tram to Place de Brouckère, in the heart of the shopping district, or some other landmark. I sauntered up and down the streets, savoring a warm *gaufre* from a waffle stand, ordering a *croque-monsieur* (grilled ham and cheese) in a stylish sandwich bar, indulging in a bag of *pralinés* from one of the countless chocolate shops. When it rained, which was fairly often, I could always retreat to one of the city's many *galeries*—covered shopping arcades, some dating from the 19th century. I admired the Grand'Place and its guildhalls, Brussels' testimonial to medieval grandeur. Along with other tourists, I chuckled at the statue of the Manneken Pis, the little boy who, according to legend, saved the Grand'Place from a fire by peeing on the flames. Soon I was setting specific goals for the day: the Atomium in Heysel, the Parc du Cinquantenaire, the Ixelles ponds, a special art gallery exhibit, or even a visit to a museum. I especially liked the Musée d'Art Ancien et Moderne (the modern part only), and the Musée Royal de l'Afrique Centrale (suitably anthropological) in Tervuren. It wasn't long before I moved with a native's ease within the roughly triangular area formed by Place de la Monnaie, Place Louise, and the Arts-Loi tram stop. Everything I could possibly need lay right there at my feet; and the best part was, I didn't have to spend a lot of money to enjoy it.

Brussels brought a series of revelations, none better than Belgian cuisine, which stood in stark contrast to the plain German fare Allen and I had gotten used to:

Fondu au fromage: small, deep-fried squares of melted cheese
Waterzooï: chicken cooked in a cream sauce with finely chopped vegetables
Filet américain: raw hamburger meat mixed with egg and spices
Jambon d'Ardennes: smoked ham from the Ardennes region
Tomates aux crevettes: tomatoes stuffed with tiny shrimp and mayonnaise
Boudin de Liège: blood sausage mixed with herbs
Sole à l'Ostendaise: sole in a white wine sauce
Carbonnade flamande: beef braised in beer
Lotte aux poireaux: monkfish with leeks in cream sauce
Lapin à la gueuze: rabbit cooked in beer
Gratin d'endives: endives wrapped in ham slices and baked in a creamy cheese sauce
Asperges à la Flamande: white asparagus served with egg and melted butter
Moules: mussels prepared in dozens of ways

Although I wasn't fond of mussels, I enjoyed watching Allen dig into heaping platefuls of the shellfish, cooked on a bed of celery, onion and parsley. Depending on his mood, he ordered them *au gratin,* or smothered with garlic, or soaked in white wine. Going out to eat is a national pastime in Belgium. That is how we discovered the restaurant Vincent, on Rue des Dominicains in the Ilot Sacré quarter. A history teacher at BAS, a long-time resident of Brussels familiar with its best addresses, invited us there one evening. An open, glassed-in kitchen at the front of the establishment enabled patrons to view how food was prepared before it arrived at their table.

Naturally, eating out in Brussels could turn into an expensive proposition. But since our apartment was located only steps from Place Dumon, a self-contained slice of gastronomical heaven, we didn't feel deprived in the least. The square had every specialty shop you could ask for: a *boucherie*, where we purchased freshly prepared *filet américain*, best spread on a baguette; a couple of bakeries; a tiny *fromagerie*, always packed with customers; a wine shop; a *poissonnerie* that didn't even smell of fish; a greengrocer's; a small supermarket at the corner; and the ubiquitous pub, or *estaminet*, with the words Stella Artois written in bold letters on the façade, which led Allen to believe that was the name of the pub, when in fact it referred to one of Belgium's most famous beers. Other conveniences included a *librairie-papeterie* (bookstore-cum-stationery), a *mercerie* (notions), a tobacconist's shop selling newspapers and magazines from around the world, a *fleuriste*, a five-and-ten selling cheap umbrellas and old ladies' stockings. Three times a week the square became host to a bustling open-air market. Laden with bags of groceries, Allen and I would treat ourselves to a paper cone of divine, twice-fried (makes all the difference) *frites mayonnaise* from the snack truck parked at the top of Val des Seigneurs.

Food, in other words, was everywhere. So was art.

One of my favorite haunts was the *quartier du Sablon*, with its artsy-craftsy boutiques and beguiling art galleries. Even the Gothic church overlooking the Place du Grand Sablon held a certain charm. It was as if I had been deprived of art and now needed to make up for it. When the weather permitted, I liked to sit in the Petit Sablon park with a copy of the Herald Tribune and something to munch on. One such afternoon, I came upon the Conservatoire Royal de Musique on Rue de la Régence. Since moving to Germany, I had stopped playing the piano, for the simple reason that we didn't have one. But surely the conservatory had practice rooms for students. That evening I told Allen about my plan, outlining its benefits, the joy I would feel at being able to play again. Allen, amused, gave his blessing.

The only class I could enroll in without taking an entrance examination was *solfège*, a deadly subject, but intent on becoming a member of the Conservatoire I filled out the forms anyway, paid the small fee, and agreed to be vaccinated against tuberculosis, as required. Once a week I attended class with a dozen or so students, and tried to overcome my dislike of *dictées musicales*. When I found out that practice rooms were only available to serious students, i.e. those taking master classes, I was disappointed. Someone suggested trying a music store on Rue de Livourne, near Avenue Louise.

Pianos Hanlet's impressive showroom displayed lustrous instruments in a variety of styles and finishes. The routine was simple: upon entering this musical shrine, you walked past the tempting grands, bore left into a dark, narrow hallway, where fragments of music rose from behind closed doors, and went to your assigned room. For an hour, or longer if you had the time and money, you escaped into your own little world.

Allen bought a car, a used Volkswagen Squareback, which meant that weekends could now be spent traveling farther afield: the Forêt de Soignes, favored by horseback riders; Waterloo, site of the historic 1815 battle between Napoleon and the Duke of Wellington; Antwerp's Grote Markt; Ghent and its ornate guild houses; Bruges' picturesque canals; the coastal town of Ostend; Leuven, the seat of Belgium's oldest university, where I felt an inexplicable kinship with ambling students. During our jaunts outside Brussels, the officially bilingual but mostly French-speaking capital, we became aware of the linguistic and cultural rift that existed between the Dutch-speaking provinces and the French-speaking ones. In rural Flanders especially, I found that speaking French got me nowhere; on the contrary, it was a source of irritation to *les Flamands* who either ignored me or answered in English. That suited Allen fine. He had picked up a few words of French, but preferred to stick to English.

Living in a monarchy held an aura of mystery. Whenever we passed the Royal Castle in Laeken, where King Baudouin and his wife Fabiola resided, we tried to imagine what life behind the thick walls and dense foliage was like. Years ahead of me, Queen Fabiola had attended the same school in Lausanne. To think that I had actually paced the same halls, eaten in the same dining room, used the same *toilettes* as the Queen of Belgium! (Not that it got me a royal audience, mind you.) Nearby stood the Chinese Pavilion and Japanese Pagoda, both commissioned by King Leopold II shortly after the Paris Universal Exhibition in 1900. That Leopold, by the way, was the same king known for his brutal colonization of the former Belgian Congo. At the time, my knowledge of history was shoddy at best, despite years of Catholic schooling. All I knew was that Brussels, unlike other cities I had lived in, had a sizable African population and that those regal women draped in colorful dresses with matching head wraps gave the Belgian capital a nice, exotic feel.

We took advantage of Belgium's proximity to Holland and went on holiday there. Rotterdam impressed us with its modernist architecture, while Delft looked just like the famous blue-and-white porcelain depictions. We spent a day in Amsterdam, where we visited Anne Frank's House, the Van Gogh Museum, and the red-light district, a major tourist attraction. Heading north towards Friesland, we took delight in the picture-perfect landscape: windmills, fields of tulips, tidy little houses with lace curtains hanging in the windows. In Alkmaar, we watched strapping Dutchmen sell wheels of golden-hued cheese in the town square. We stopped in Volendam, an old fishing village on the Markermeer near Edam. The open-air Zuiderzee Museum in Enkhuizen, where people walk around in traditional garb and clogs, gave visitors a glimpse of an earlier, simpler lifestyle. We drove on the Afsluitdijk, the long, wind-swept dike that crosses the Zuiderzee, a large, shallow inlet of the North Sea. The flat Netherlands, about twenty percent of which lie below sea level, made Belgium look positively hilly.

Having a car also enabled us to drive down to SHAPE (Supreme Headquarters Allied Powers Europe) once a month to load up on American goods at the PX, a vast converted hangar in the midst of the Hainaut countryside, near Chièvres. In the wintertime the road from Brussels, via Nivelles and Mons, was often treacherous in the fog, characteristic of Belgium's mild, maritime climate.

We had met a wonderful group of teachers with whom we socialized a lot. They were, for the most part, mildly eccentric American expatriates with a distinct preference for the European way of life. They traveled extensively, went to the ballet, the opera, concerts, plays, art exhibits, flea markets, upscale restaurants. Many of them had become gourmet cooks, plying us with frequent *dégustations* of their latest culinary creations. Some, fluent in French, straddled their biculturalism with ease.

It was, therefore, hard to accept that Allen's contract would not be renewed at the end of the school year. Nothing to do with his performance, you understand. It was simply a question of him being a local hire, just as had been the case in Ludwigsburg, with no guarantee of employment beyond the term of his contract.

Maman was spending the summer in St. Luc, and invited us there while Papa was still in Berne. We took the train to Basel, where we briefly visited our faithful group of friends, and continued south towards the Alps. In St. Luc, Maman was waiting in front of the post office where the yellow postal bus dropped us off. We embraced warmly.

At the chalet, a traditional cheese fondue, with *viande séchée*, gherkins, onions, and a bottle of Kirsch, awaited us. Allen impressed Maman with his knowledge of fondue etiquette. He knew the cheese had to be stirred in a figure eight motion; he knew about the *coup du milieu*—the shot of Kirsch served midway through a fondue; he knew that if men inadvertently dropped their bread in the pot, they had to buy a bottle a wine, and when that happened to the ladies, well, all that was required of them was a kiss all around. What Allen learned that day was how to enjoy *la religieuse* (literally: the nun), the crispy bit of burning cheese you scrape off the bottom of the pot. The conversation at the rustic dining room table flowed easily, with Allen engaging Maman in a number of topics that immediately set off an animated discussion. I watched, glad that they got along so well. My brother, his wife and their young son were vacationing in the *mazot* my father had renovated for them below the main house. The following day, after the introductions, we all went for a walk to La Barmaz, a lookout point at the edge of the forest with sweeping views of the Rhône Valley.

Back at the house, we sat on the balcony and admired the mighty Matterhorn in the distance. Someone brought up the lack of communication between my father and me.

"This whole thing," JC said suddenly, "has gone on long enough. It's plain stupid. I'm going to call him right now to tell him we're coming over tomorrow."

My brother's stand surprised me. I glanced at serene, noncommittal Allen.

"I don't know if it's such a good idea," I said, as JC rose to make the call. "What if he refuses? Or worse, he agrees to see us and makes a terrible scene?"

"Look, you and Allen are leaving for the States in two weeks. Perfect opportunity to say goodbye. Plus he gets a chance to meet your husband."

"He knows I'm married, right?" I asked Maman.

"Of course."

"Okay, let's do it then." We strained to hear what my brother was saying on the phone. He came back a few minutes later, looking pleased.

"Well?"

"It's all settled. He's expecting us for dinner tomorrow evening."

The next day my mother, who would not be joining us, waved us off from the top of the unpaved driveway. The ride to Berne was uneventful and mostly silent, except for the gurgling sounds emanating from my nephew, who soon fell asleep. At the Roschi, we crammed into the elevator, rang the doorbell.

"*Bonsoir!*" Papa said expansively as he opened the door. "Come in, come in!" He bent down and pinched his grandson's cheek, fussing over him. He shook my brother's hand, kissed my sister-in-law, and proceeded to ignore Allen and me. Incredulous, I stepped forward and said hello.

"And this is Allen, my husband."

At last my father made eye contact with me. He didn't hug me, nor did he shake Allen's hand. Right then and there, I had the urge to flee. But Allen gave me a nudge and we stepped inside.

Papa had cooked spaghetti with tomato sauce. We all followed him to the kitchen where he put the finishing touches to the meal, all the while chatting in French with my brother and his wife. Feeling left out, I took Allen to my old room, which Maman had appropriated after my departure. I was about to show him the rest of the apartment when we heard a loud crash in the kitchen, followed by exclamations and tears. We made a beeline for the kitchen and in the ensuing chaos—my nephew had found a jar of his grandmother's homemade jam in a low cupboard and dropped it—Allen took the toddler's hand and, carefully avoiding the broken glass, left the scene. The three of us disappeared from sight until dinner was served.

At the dining room table, Papa sat in his usual spot. Realizing there would be no buffer zone between him and me, I discreetly moved my chair closer to Allen's.

During the meal Papa, my brother and his wife entertained each other with lively tales from the rarified world of medicine. I wondered why JC wasn't changing the topic. It had been his idea to come here, and now Papa was deliberately ignoring me, which was to be expected, but also Allen, which was bloody rude, and my brother wasn't doing anything about it. Just as I was about to signal my discontent to Allen with my foot, my father looked at his son-in-law.

"What is your university degree?" he asked in English.

Allen almost choked on the forkful of spaghetti he was about to swallow. He finished chewing, wiped his mouth and smiled.

"I have a bachelor's."

My father took a swig of red wine.

"In what subject?"

"Business education."

Silence.

Papa turned to JC and resumed his conversation in French. I decided at that moment that we would leave after dinner.

As soon as the last crumb was off everyone's plate, I stood up and started to gather the dirty dishes. With efficiency and purpose I rinsed the plates and stacked them into the dishwasher. My sister-in-law went to change her son. JC helped clear the table. Allen had vanished. I went looking for him and stopped dead in my tracks. Was I dreaming? My husband and my father, sitting in the *fumoir*, chatting like old friends. Allen, reclining on the sofa with his legs crossed, smiled and spoke softly; Papa laughed. Laughed! I think music was playing in the background. Excuse me, I wanted to say, but am I missing something here? Didn't *you*, Dad, just insult Allen at the dinner table? And why on earth would *you*, Allen, want to talk to someone who just insulted you?

Later on, after Allen had convinced me to stay the night, he described the genesis of their conversation. He had asked Papa about his passion for classical music and my father had responded warmly. Went on to disclose how difficult a decision he'd had to face at eighteen, when he chose medicine over music. He had never regretted his choice, but music would always remain an integral part of his life.

"Unbelievable . . . ."

"Actually, it's very simple," said Allen. "It has to do with psychology. People, no matter who they are, love to talk about themselves. All you have to do is ask them about something they're passionate about and they'll open up."

"I couldn't do it."

"Sure you could."

"Not with my father."

"All you have to do is listen."

"All I know is that he never told me any of that stuff, about having to make a choice between music and medicine when he was eighteen. But he told you."

Allen had a way of convincing people who seemed least likely to be convinced. JC had offered, if things got out of hand, to drop us off at the Berne train station; he and his wife were driving to Zurich, where they lived, that evening. But when Allen spoke to me—*it's only for one night, Mona, first thing tomorrow morning we'll take the train back to Brussels*—I relented. We brought our bag to JC's old room and said goodnight, formally, to my father. Once the door was closed I felt safe in Allen's arms, the two of us squeezed in the single bed of my brother's youth.

The next morning, as I was coming out of the bathroom, Papa greeted me in the hallway.

"Good morning."

"Good morning."

Pause.

"I guess you'll be off soon."

I nodded.

"So what do you do in Brussels all day, besides being a housewife?'

"Well . . . no, I do a lot of things, I . . . ."

But Papa had made his point. He turned and walked away.

I rushed to my brother's room where Allen was getting dressed, and told him to hurry up.

Chapter Six: USA

Bangor, Maine: refueling stop and my first taste of America. Allen and I walked around the small airport, glad to stretch our legs. A crowd of travelers carrying cardboard boxes jostled against us. *Fresh Live Maine Lobsters*, signs proclaimed everywhere. We had, it seemed, landed in the lobster capital of the USA. Taking off again, we swept over rich, green forests interspersed with languid, meandering rivers and lakes, occasional settlements. From up above, it looked very different from the geometrically aligned, neatly ploughed fields of my country. Then, in the distance, we made out the skyscrapers of New York City. Shivers of excitement ran down my spine.

Kennedy Airport bustled with people speaking all sorts of languages and sporting a variety of clothes, builds, skin tones. At the baggage carousel, I was introduced to Allen's mother, Helen, petite, blonde, wearing glasses and a big smile; and his father, Harry, a big bear of a man, open arms welcoming his foreign daughter-in-law. I went to the ladies' room only to find it dirty, but what did it matter? I was peeing *in America*. Hurrah!

In the parking lot I was struck by the size of my in-laws' Oldsmobile. "It's as big as a boat!"

As we drove south to Philadelphia I counted the number of lanes on the highway: five in each direction. How could a highway have ten lanes? Unheard of in Switzerland. While Allen and his parents chatted, I took in the passing scenery. Huge suspension bridges. Litter on the side of the road. Stucco homes. Towering apartment buildings. Dilapidated warehouses. Oil refineries. After the urban sprawl, a bit of greenery. Oversize billboards. Shopping malls. Northeast Philly. Large Street, which should really be called

Long Street because it goes on forever. Harry parked the car in front of a block of brick row houses with gabled roofs, all exactly the same except for variations in awnings, front doors, flowerbeds. Helen led the way up the steps, opened something called a screen door, and showed me into a living room furnished with a green sofa, television set, and large recliner.

"Make yourself at home, honey," Helen said, "I'm going to get the food ready."

She went into the kitchen. Allen and his father brought in the suitcases.

"Let's put all this upstairs in your room."

I followed them to the second floor, where I took a quick look around: Harry and Helen's bedroom, our bedroom, a third, smaller room and the bathroom, decorated in grey and burgundy tile, with matching towels.

"This is a charming house."

"You like it? Good. Stay as long as you want."

I loved everything American. The way people spoke (much broader than the Brits), how they walked (with confidence) and dressed (quite casually). The convenience of all-night shopping, the friendliness of salespeople, the return policy in retail stores, the size of appliances. The freedom to do exactly as you pleased. (Quite a departure from life in Nuremberg, that.)

My in-laws were kind and generous. Helen gave us her Sears and Gimbels credit cards and told us to go shopping. When Harry wasn't using the car (his wife didn't drive), Allen borrowed it to show me around the area. To go downtown we had to pass through poor neighborhoods, populated for the most part, I noticed, by blacks. Why was there poverty in America? Wasn't this the richest nation on earth? How could there be such a gap between my in-laws' neighborhood (solidly middle-class) and others in a clear state of disrepair (and surely breeding despair among its dwellers)? At the opposite end of the socio-economic spectrum, in the heart of the city, stood Rittenhouse Square, symbol of Philadelphia's *haute société*, and further west the Main Line, site of the many mansions of privilege. I was surprised by what I saw, but having been told to keep my wits about me at all times and to avoid "certain neighborhoods," I learned to carry an invisible armor that would, hopefully, act as a deterrent. *Never look like you're lost* became my motto. Walk with confidence (just like the natives), know where you are going (or pretend that you do), and don't make eye contact with "suspicious-looking" characters on the street or while riding the subway. Allen took me to see some of the city's landmarks: the Liberty Bell, Independence Hall, Society Hill, a historic district near Penn's Landing lined with small, narrow red-brick townhouses in the Colonial style. This section was a showcase for successful urban renewal and, with its pedestrian-friendly streets, old-fashioned streetlights, offbeat shops and outdoor cafés, it reminded me a bit of Europe.

But our sightseeing days were numbered as Allen had to find a job. As for me, I had been accepted at Temple University, where I planned to study anthropology.

The first time I set foot in a supermarket in Philadelphia, on a Sunday no less, culture shock set in when I came upon the aisle with the salad dressings. I stood in awe. Having grown up with one variety—Maman's homemade vinaigrette—I wasn't prepared for the selection of bottled dressings in front of me: French, Italian, Creamy Italian, Russian, Thousand Island, Blue Cheese, Catalina, Ranch, Caesar, Oil and Vinegar.

"I'm going to try every single one of them."

"That will take a while."

"However long it takes."

A teaching job materialized, as Allen had predicted, but not in Northeast Philly. The high school that offered him a position, Interboro in Prospect Park, was located in the southwestern suburbs. We bought a Gremlin on credit (my first exposure to the all-American creed *Buy Now, Pay Later*) and found an apartment in a recently completed building on East Chester Pike in Ridley Park, a working-class neighborhood.

Allen and I, excited about furnishing our first apartment together, purchased a queen-size bed, a dining room set, and our very own dishes. We put up curtains, artwork, and filled the closets with fresh linens and new clothes—everything was so cheap here! I praised American ingenuity in daily encounters with built-in closets, garbage disposals, screens, air conditioning. The light and airy laundry room on the first floor was a welcome improvement over the Laundromat we used to go to in Fürth.

Temple's campus, at Broad and Montgomery, formed an academic enclave in the midst of one of those neighborhoods I was advised to avoid. As a daytime commuter student, I didn't really need to worry about safety; nevertheless, I developed a keen sense of where not to venture. The university had given me two years' worth of credits towards a Bachelor's, one year for the *Maturité* and another for my coursework in Basel. That first semester I took two classes in anthropology, one in French poetry, one in music.

For entertainment we socialized with Allen's friends and relatives, most of whom lived in the Philadelphia area. Helen, an accomplished cook, invited us often for splendid meals, and sent us home with plastic containers filled with leftovers (had word gotten out that I was a bad cook?). The City of Brotherly Love offered a number of interesting places to visit: Ben Franklin's house, the Art Museum, the Rodin Museum, Germantown, Wissahickon Creek in Fairmount Park. Allen and I toured Pennsylvania

Dutch country, where we stuffed ourselves with Amish specialties, including shoofly pie. We chuckled at the odd names given to certain towns around Lancaster: Intercourse, Bird-in-Hand, Paradise. In the spring we drove down to Washington to see the cherry blossoms and visited the Lincoln and Jefferson Memorials, the Smithsonian, the National Air and Space Museum. We spent a weekend with Allen's younger brother, fresh out of journalism school, and his wife at their apartment in Virginia Beach. But the city I liked best of all was New York, although we didn't have the opportunity to go there frequently.

Allen taught, I studied. An outsider looking in through the window of our apartment in Ridley Park might well have concluded: nothing much going on here. Not a bad assessment. Allen graded papers, I wrote papers; he made up tests for his students, I took tests. Although I had befriended a couple of male students at Temple, I never invited them home. I didn't attend school parties, or seek to be popular. I went to class, borrowed books from Paley Library, and went home to my husband at the end of the day.

The man who would be the greatest influence on me during that period was my adviser, Professor Bredahl-Petersen, a Dane with a penchant for caustic wit and a special interest in North Atlantic Settlements and Norse Culture. I drank in his every word at lectures. When he introduced Claude Lévi-Strauss' structuralism to us, I became an instant and fervent follower of the French anthropologist's theories, at least the few bits I understood, like his insistence that the "savage" mind of so-called primitive people was not inferior to the "civilized" mind of Western society. I envisioned doing fieldwork in Papua New Guinea, or living among the Yanomamö of South America.

Ruth Benedict's *Patterns of Culture,* Chinua Achebe's *Things Fall Apart,* Margaret Mead's *Coming of Age in Samoa,* Peter Worsley's *The Trumpet Shall Sound* were books I particularly enjoyed. The more exotic the tribe, the more admirable in my eyes. I chafed at Western civilization's arrogance while enjoying its privileges: the freedom to express myself, to shop at midnight, to choose my own spouse, to decide whether or not to have children, to study.

Early in '76 Allen applied to DOD. That had been our plan all along. We were both committed to finish the school year in Philadelphia, but eager to move again, anywhere in the world. The application process, requiring masses of paperwork, notarized statements, interviews, was long and arduous. We wouldn't know for months.

In my second semester, Prof. Bredahl-Petersen had taught a course entitled "Peoples of the North Atlantic Littoral." He had done fieldwork among Scandinavian fishermen and, as my mentor, would have liked me to follow in his footsteps. I didn't know yet what I wanted to do once I obtained my degree. Faraway destinations beckoned.

We heard from DOD a month after I graduated. There was an opening in Keflavík, Iceland. Allen had to give an answer within forty-eight hours.

Iceland? We took out the atlas and looked for a small island in the North Atlantic. Neither of us knew anything about the country, except that it had geysers and the capital was Reykjavík. We danced around the room. It was what we had wished for. Not Iceland exactly, but to be living in another part of the world.

"Iceland?" exclaimed my adviser. "But that's wonderful! Now you can do your thesis on the Icelandic fishermen."

I was swept along by his enthusiasm. Over the next few weeks, we met at the rambling old house he shared with his wife in West Philadelphia to devise a systematic approach to my proposed fieldwork: purpose of research, selection of respondents, observing and interviewing participants, collection and analysis of data, recording findings, and writing it all up in a coherent manner. Armed with the names of two Icelandic contacts and pages of scribbled notes, I was now ready to put what I had learned into practice.

In the whirlwind of pre-departure activity I decided to pay a brief visit to my parents. I had been in contact with Maman during those two years, sending her copies of my college essays which she kindly praised. With Papa there had been no communication. On the rare occasions that I called home, I prayed that he wouldn't be the one answering the phone.

Allen had to stay behind and wait for our visas. The movers would pick up our furniture from Large Street, where we had relocated at the expiration of our lease, and deliver it, two months later, in Keflavík. And this time we were traveling in style, i.e. at government expense.

I flew to Zurich and took the train to Berne, where Maman met me at the *Hauptbahnhof.* My reunion with Papa was awkward at first. We kept the conversation anodyne, and an unspoken truce went into effect. I began to relax. That is, until I told my parents one evening that I wouldn't be joining them in St. Luc: I preferred to stay in Berne, meeting up with old friends.

Papa took it badly.

"What's wrong with you? Of course, you're coming with us tomorrow!"

I shook my head.

Maman, already in her nightgown, sat on a chair in the hallway.

"Look," she said quietly to her husband, averting her eyes from his mounting fury. "Let her do what she wants. She's an adult now."

"I don't care what she is! She's coming with us to the chalet."

He stood so close to me that I thought he was going to slap me. Instead, he pulled my hair, twice.

I took a step back and sneered.

"What are you doing?" Maman asked Papa, her voice heavy with sadness. "Do you really want to drive your daughter away again? Because that's what's going to happen."

"It's too bad," I told my father with surprising calmness, *"tu as l'intelligence du cerveau, mais pas l'intelligence du cœur."* Loosely translated: You've got brains but no heart.

He glared at me, unsure of his next move. Then he marched off to his bedroom and slammed the door.

Maman and I retreated to my brother's old room to discuss the implications of what had just happened. She asked me to reconsider my decision. I didn't promise anything. We agreed to sleep on it.

The next day I rose early and knocked on Papa's door.

"Who is it?"

"It's me. Can I come in?"

My father, looking very small and vulnerable, lay on his back with the sheets pulled up to his neck.

"Bonjour, papa," I said cheerfully. "Did you sleep well?"

"I didn't sleep a wink." And he began to sob.

I kneeled by the bed and kissed him on the forehead.

"It's okay . . ." I patted his hand. ". . . it's okay to cry . . . ."

He blew his nose loudly.

"I've decided to come up to the chalet."

A ghost of a smile appeared on his face.

"C'est vrai?"

"Yes, it's true."

Later I told my mother I had never loved my father more than at that very moment, when he proved, beyond a doubt, that he did have a heart.

Chapter Seven: ICELAND

*L*and of contrasts. Volcanoes and glaciers. Geysers, waterfalls, hot springs and lava rocks. More sheep than people. No trees. As the story goes, the Vikings landed here over a thousand years ago and, finding it much to their liking (there were trees back then), they decided to trick newcomers into traveling further west, to a fertile place named Greenland. In reality, Greenland has far more ice than Iceland, which is really green.

Had the early settlers wanted to be perfectly accurate, they would have called this place Windland. Gale, we found out the hard way, was the country's dominant feature.

Second thing we noticed: it wasn't as cold as we had expected. Even though the island lies just south of the Arctic Circle, its climate is relatively mild, thanks to the Gulf Stream.

Third, the landscape was forbidding, almost otherworldly.

We were definitely not in Kansas anymore.

Keflavík International Airport, the site of the U.S. Naval Air Station, is where we deplaned. American military personnel shared the space with ruddy-cheeked people speaking an incomprehensible tongue. We became aware of a foul smell in the air. Not the smell of freshly caught fish, or even rotten fish. What we were smelling, a sympathetic Yank informed us, came from the Keflavík fish-processing factory down the road, and there would be no escape from it, so we might as well get used to it. Oh, that stench! If the wind blew a certain way, it could kill plans for a romantic evening.

Allen and I were given a key to our billeting quarters, temporary accommodations in the bachelor housing section, until we found an apartment off base—as civilians, we were not entitled to base housing. The room was basic, a built-in incentive to get out of there fast. Buying a car became a top priority: local taxis were expensive, and we couldn't rely on the kindness of others to drive us around indefinitely. We snapped up a used Fiat 128, despite evidence of rust on the body. Next, we saw a partially furnished flat that I insisted we rent immediately. Allen had reservations about it—too small and old-fashioned, and not private enough (the stairs leading up to the flat were accessible only from the landlord's ground floor apartment). But I wanted to get off base so badly I didn't listen. We took out a monthly lease, and before our furniture arrived from the States three weeks later we had moved out to a modern two-bedroom with private entrance and balcony (not that we would ever use it) in nearby Njardvík.

Culture shock began in earnest once we settled in Njardvík. So many things to figure out and no language skills to help the process along. *Godan daginn* (hello) and *takk fyrir* (thank you)—that was pretty much the extent of our vocabulary in those early days. I recognized the Germanic root in many Icelandic words, but to be able to pronounce them correctly was another matter. At the small local supermarket I tried to buy recognizable foods like frozen shrimp, eggs, milk, chocolate. Thanks to tips from teachers who had lived in Iceland for years, I unearthed a bakery—it had no window displays, no signs to identify it as such. The flat, foot-and-a-half long Danish filled with almond paste and topped with pink or yellow icing, depending on what day of the week it was, would become the staple of my Icelandic life.

At the first opportunity Allen and I drove to Reykjavík. Surprise number one: the road to the capital, some fifty miles away, was paved! Surprise number two: once you left Njardvík, there was nothing but lava fields on one side of the road and the ocean on the other until you reached Hafnarfjördur, where a large aluminum factory signaled the end of the rugged, desolate landscape.

Reykjavík was like no other city we had visited before. A fishing town of approximately 90,000 inhabitants—almost half of the entire country's population—it sat on a wide bay surrounded by majestic mountains. The air was crisp, the sea, clear blue; the streets were as immaculate as those in Switzerland. A handful of newly planted trees. A large duck pond, Lake Tjörnin, where birds flocked. As for the architecture, it was mostly functional, the uniformity of design accentuated by whimsically painted houses adorned with red, blue, or green roofs.

We parked the car and started walking. First on Austurstræti, with its touristy shops selling Icelandic woolens in various shades of beige, brown and grey, sheepskins, silver jewelry, wood sculptures (where did they find the wood, we wondered), ceramics, postcards. We continued on Bankastræti, which turns into Laugavegur, the city's main artery. The view from the top of the hill wasn't bad: Reykjavík Harbour with its fleet of trawlers anchored in the calm bay and snow-capped Mr. Esja in the distance. (The famed Cod War with Great Britain, over Iceland's decision to extend its fishing limits to two hundred miles from the coastline, had ended in June of that year.)

We ate our first Icelandic meal in a tiny café: *smorrebrod* topped with *hangikjöt* (smoked lamb) and a Scandinavian version of *salade russe* (peas, carrots and diced potatoes in mayonnaise). Few people spoke English away from the tourist spots, so Allen and I struggled with our order. I, for one, didn't want any shark meat, sheep's brains, ram's testicles, or cod. We sampled *skyr* for dessert, a mix between yogurt and cream cheese, similar to the German *Quark,* served plain or flavored with berries.

We had been told by many Americans that Icelandic hot dogs were out of this world, especially the ones from Baejarins Bestu, a stand at the intersection of Posthusstræti and Tryggvagata. Indeed, they were tasty. Icelandic *pylsur* are made mostly from lamb; but what differentiates them from our basic dogs is the fact that the buns are steamed and filled with mustard, ketchup, crunchy fried onions, raw onions, and *remuladi* (remoulade sauce). To get the works, you quickly learn how to say *eina med öllu* ("one with everything").

This being late August, we could still enjoy long hours of daylight, though not quite the full effect of the midnight sun. (To keep their bedrooms dark despite the outside light, Icelanders fit all windows with heavy black drapes.) Allen and I opted *not* to take a dip in Reykjavík's outdoor municipal pool, open all year and heated by geothermal water. Geothermal energy is so plentiful in Iceland that it has been tapped to heat homes and office buildings, an inexpensive and non-polluting way to keep the population warm. In 874 AD Ingólfur Arnarson, Iceland's first Viking settler (Irish monks lived on the island before, but left when the Vikings started to arrive), named the area Smokey Bay for all the steam that rose from natural hot water springs there.

Allen loved his teaching job at A.T. Mahan High School. I drove him every morning, stopping at the gate on the way in, and drove back off base, always hoping that the guards wouldn't search the car for smuggled merchandise. As civilians living off base, we were allowed to purchase a limited amount of American goods on base each month, as they carried a high resale value among the locals, especially booze and cigarettes. At first we complied, handing over receipts for inspection and smiling at the poker-faced guards. Over time we developed an elaborate routine that did not, shall we say, involve full disclosure. We never engaged in contraband, of course, but merely amused ourselves by devising ways to circumvent the strict regulations. For instance, we opened boxes of tissues or dried food so they wouldn't look new, we hid wine bottles in furry boots, we—but enough said.

Our apartment was cozy; I knew my way around Keflavík; it was time to investigate those Icelandic fishermen. One morning, after dropping Allen off, I drove to Reykjavík to meet with one of Bredahl-Petersen's contacts, a retired teacher, charming, cultured, and suffering from gout. His wife offered us coffee and cookies, and we talked about my proposed research. Although my host didn't exactly discourage me, he cautioned me that I would find it difficult to interview fishermen. "The Icelandic people," he explained, "tend to be reserved, unless they've been drinking, that is, then you'll find them to be quite boisterous. But they aren't likely to open up to a complete stranger, fishermen even less so."

I thanked him for the advice and, map in hand, headed for the harbor. If truth be told, I took one whiff and turned around. Was it realistic, I asked myself on the way back, to conduct research among fishermen who wouldn't be keen on talking to me anyway? But perhaps I had been too hasty. I would go and talk to the fishermen in Keflavík.

The Keflavík fishermen never stood a chance. As luck would have it, the moment I chose for my foray is when the fish factory decided to emit its characteristic odor. Nearly gagging, I retreated to the apartment and considered my options. If I wasn't going to do research, then at least I should learn Old Norse, so I could read the Sagas and Eddas in the language of the Vikings. I went back to Reykjavík the next day, this time to speak to someone at the University of Iceland. I parked the Fiat in the semi-circle facing an austere, grayish-brown building and sauntered up the stairs.

The news on that front wasn't good. The only class of Icelandic taught in English started in the late afternoon. That would mean driving back and forth on the dark, half-deserted road during the winter months. I had envisioned taking day classes and spending my evenings with Allen.

I would look for a job on base. But working at the U.S. Naval Air Station wasn't as easy as all that. Jobs went to American citizens first, next to Icelanders, and last to Third Nationals. Once again, being Swiss put me at a disadvantage. Why not become an American? I had obtained a green card upon entering the country in 1974, but immigration laws required a three-year period of residency prior to being eligible for naturalization. What if I wrote a letter to immigration describing my situation? I had spent two years on American soil, and now, as a result of my husband's work, was posted to a military base overseas. Wasn't that technically U.S. soil? If so, could I apply to become a citizen while living in Iceland? To my surprise, the answer came back positive. I would have to study for the test and pay a visit to the immigration office in Philadelphia the following summer.

I started to frequent the American library on base, taking out two, three books at a time, mostly novels, and reading them at a leisurely pace. As daylight receded, I borrowed more and read obsessively. Each morning I'd swing by the bakery to pick up my daily ration of pastry, go back home and curl up with a book until it was time to pick up Allen. I made a few trips to the capital in search of culture, but Reykjavík was not Brussels. How often could I admire Asmundur Sveinsson's outdoor sculptures? The weather, too, was becoming a hindrance. Flat tires were a regular occurrence, caused in part by rocks and potholes, but also by the wear and tear of our studded tires, required for better traction in the snow. Thankfully, Allen had shown me how to change a flat when it happened the first time. Getting dirt and grease on my clothes didn't matter anymore since I had adopted the Icelandic attire of choice: jeans and a navy blue parka.

Allen and I had taken advantage of the last days of summer to visit some of the country's most famous sites: Thingvellir, the birthplace of the *Althing* or Viking-age parliament, a sprawling, treeless rift valley that elicited a laconic *That's it?* from me; the Great Geysir area, teeming with geysers, hot springs and mud pools, where the Strokkur spouted up several feet every few minutes; the rainbow-misted, two-tier Gullfoss ("Golden Falls") waterfall, one of Iceland's largest. Closer to Keflavík, we toured the Reykjanes Peninsula, glimpsing the Blue Lagoon from behind a wire fence because it just happened to be closed that day (the lagoon, whose popularity grew in the 1980's, long after we had left, was created by chance when engineers at the Svartsengi Geothermal Plant diverted run-off water from the plant after heat exchange and found that the hot, unpolluted, mineral-rich waters had healing powers); Krisuvík, with its steam vents and solfaratas; Grindavík, yet another fishing village.

Iceland's offerings were, for the most part, geological, and held little interest for me. The wonders of nature had yet to sway me—I was twenty-five and a city girl at heart. Nonetheless, walks on the windswept beach at Sandgerdi became, by default, our preferred form of relaxation on weekends. Allen collected seashells; I watched seals lazing about on glistening rocks. On occasion we saw movies at the Andrews Theater on base, where people stood en masse when the Star-Spangled Banner came on (I could never understand the reason for this: the US was not, after all, England, where people still sang God Save the Queen at the drop of a hat); or we had dinner at the Top of the Rock, the enlisted club. One evening Allen and I got dressed up and went to the Symphony in Reykjavík to hear Vladimir Ashkenazy, whose wife was Icelandic. The hall's overhead lights weren't turned off during the performance and we wondered if that was a malfunction or a local custom.

By now winter, with its four hours of daylight, was in full swing, and we were discovering just how jolly the Icelanders could be. In our apartment building loud, all-night parties ended only when every opened bottle of liquor had been finished, as tradition would have it, and a few empty ones had been flung over the balconies for good measure. In a bizarre attempt to control drunkenness, the government had prohibited the sale of alcoholic beer. Instead, people drank the more potent stuff, like *brennivín* (Icelandic schnapps) and vodka, which only got them drunk sooner.

We didn't befriend any Icelanders. Distrust seemed to reign between the locals and the Americans, who complained that the Icelanders were only too happy to take their money but didn't want their presence on the island. The base at Keflavík had been a source of controversy for some time. However, as Americans were keen to point out, it did provide numerous economic benefits to Iceland, which the government could not ignore. So with a few exceptions, Americans socialized among themselves, and Icelanders stuck to their own. Small acts of sabotage, like siphoning gas out of American cars, took place fairly often. Since everything, except fish, sheep and geothermal energy, had to be imported, the cost of living was high, thus breeding resentment towards U.S. personnel with access to cheap goods through the PX and commissary. The majority of Icelanders, a fiercely proud and independent people, did not like the fact that their international airport sat in the middle of a foreign military installation.

We decided not to stick around for Christmas and flew to London. The plane was filled with Americans suffering from island (as in small and dark island) fever, relishing the prospect of sampling all things British for a few days. That trip to England and bitter return to Keflavík convinced Allen to put in for a transfer.

The Iceland of 1976 was a far cry from the fashionable destination it has become today. It was considered a hardship assignment: a one-year tour of duty for DOD teachers. Gloomy days in January, when I drove Allen to work in the dark and picked him up several hours later in the same darkness, inched forward at their inexorable pace. The only hope we had was imminent news of our transfer, preferably to sunnier climes. As time passed and Allen's colleagues told of their futile attempts at "getting out of this godforsaken place," we began to despair.

By spring we knew. No transfers. Allen could resign, relocate to Philadelphia, and re-apply to DOD. Or he could stay another year.

* * *

The flight back to Keflavík at the end of the summer was, well, a trip. We flew out of McGuire Air Force Base in New Jersey, courtesy of Uncle Sam, sitting backwards in a converted C-141 cargo plane filled with U.S. Navy personnel. Rows of rudimentary seats facing the rear of the plane had been mounted on the floor to accommodate passengers. Due to the lack of insulation, headsets were provided to dull the deafening noise inside the aircraft. Needless to say, smiling stewardesses were not on board. Food, in the form of reconstituted eggs and stale bread, was supplied, at cost, on a self-service basis. We were halfway across the Atlantic when we felt the plane turn around. No announcement was made, but from the banter around us we gathered that the reason given was bad weather in Iceland. No one believed it. *Bad weather in Iceland? Ha, that's a good one! More likely they're having mechanical problems.* Back at McGuire, we spent the rest of the night sprawled on plastic chairs in the waiting area until our flight was called—again.

"I don't care how expensive it is," I told Allen when we finally landed in Keflavík, "next time we fly commercial."

Year Two began auspiciously. I was now a naturalized citizen. Allen and I had found another flat and were excited about our new home, a pastel-colored house on Nonvarda, a residential street in Keflavík. The landlord, his wife and their four children lived upstairs while we rented the downstairs apartment, which had large windows, an enormous living room, a tiled kitchen with plenty of cabinets, and three bedrooms. Some of Allen's colleagues wondered why we needed so much space since we didn't have children—unless (giggle) we were planning on starting a family. But the rent was affordable, the neighborhood quiet (we hoped), and our new landlords—married, we presumed, but bearing different last names—were quite personable. Iceland, following Norse tradition, uses a patronymic naming system that identifies people as the sons or daughters of their father. So, for example, Einar, son of Gunnar, becomes Einar Gunnarsson, while Sigrid, daughter of, say, another Gunnar, is called Sigrid Gunnarsdóttir. To us foreigners, this nomenclature was maddening, especially when we had to look someone up in the phone book, where people were listed by their first names.

The owners' youngest child, barely a year old, was often left in his carriage for hours on the second-floor balcony, and we privately questioned the wisdom of such a practice. We were told that leaving babies bundled up in their prams outdoors was quite common, as the Icelanders believed it promoted good health from an early age, not to mention rosy cheeks.

As a newly-minted American, I was eager to get a job. But first we had a visit from my mother, who had expressed interest in seeing Iceland. We rented a red Beetle in Reykjavík to have more flexibility, and also because the Fiat had become unreliable. Corrosion due to salty roads and damp weather had taken its toll on the undercarriage and doors, from which pieces of rusted metal fell off if they were slammed too hard. Each morning one of us had to coax the engine, pleading with it to start. Sometimes it did; other times, in true Mediterranean fashion, it wouldn't. Never buy an Italian car north of the Alps, we concluded, much too temperamental.

During her short visit Maman packed in the sights. I drove her to Reykjavík where she insisted on taking a dip in the outdoor swimming pool. By the time I picked her up an hour later, she knew she had caught a cold. We stopped at the Arbær Folk Museum, a handful of old cottages built of stone and turf. I showed her Thingvellir (which bored me even more than the first time), the Strokkur geyser, the beach at Sandgerdi. My mother, unlike me, is very much a nature lover. She marveled at the rugged lava fields, the flora sprouting in the most unlikely places, the colonies of puffins, Arctic terns and myriad other birds. On impulse we went to a horse farm and rode sturdy, gentle Icelandic ponies. One day she took a propeller plane to the Westman Islands where, in 1973, a volcanic eruption completely covered Heimaey, the only inhabited island. We wanted to explore the region around Mt. Esja, across from Reykjavík, but had to turn around because a strong wind threatened to push the VW and its occupants straight into the icy waters of Faxaflói.

Aware of my frustrations during the previous year, Maman decided that having a piano would cheer me up. After a few inquiries we ended up in Reykjavík's only piano store. We pushed open the door to the minuscule shop and there, in the narrow space, stood three gleaming, identical Yamaha uprights. I sat down to try them out. The first two were nice enough; but when my fingers hit the third piano's keyboard, magic filled the air. It sounded almost like a grand, especially when you opened the top. Incredulous, I gazed at the elegant, polished instrument while my mother arranged to have it delivered to Keflavík.

Barely able to contain my excitement, I kissed and thanked Maman. As far as we knew, those were the only three Yamahas for sale in Reykjavík, and one of them turned out to be exceptional. What was the likelihood of finding such a gem (made in Japan, shipped to Iceland from Hamburg) in this hellhole?

Allen joined us for Maman's final sightseeing trip. Our itinerary took us to Hveragerdi, where fruits, vegetables and flowers are grown year round in geothermally heated greenhouses; Selfoss; and the Skógafoss waterfall, Iceland's tallest at 200 feet. For months Allen had been talking about going to Vík to see the famous Black Beach, but I wasn't keen at all, especially not while my mother was visiting. It was chilly and overcast, and the last thing I wanted was to get stuck in this no-man's-land as night fell. But Allen insisted, and Maman wasn't about to object. So we drove on towards the coast.

I'd had a bad feeling ever since we left Skógar, and complained that Vík was too far, not to mention a pointless expedition. Allen assured me that he knew where he was going, and that we would be home before dusk.

LEAVING EUROPE

The pale midday sun had long vanished, as it often did in this subarctic part of the world, and the only sound amid the glacial outwash plains was the erratic bumping of the Volkswagen on the tortuous gravel road. A lone skua swooped up ahead, crying her sad song, and disappeared behind the rocks overhanging the sea.

"There it is," Allen exclaimed as we came to a bend in the road. He shifted into first, deftly maneuvering the steep descent towards the beach. At the foot of the hill, a mere twenty yards from the shoreline, he cut off the engine.

Maman slid into a pair of waterproof boots and buttoned her ancient fur coat. It had been, at one time, a fashionable specimen of what furriers did with mink tails; now all that remained was a worn, grayish-brown garment, flared at the bottom. Still, Maman, in her early sixties, looked as stylish as ever.

I shrugged. "Okay, we made it. Now can we please go back?"

Allen zipped up his parka.

"Might as well go and take a look since we're here."

I stared out the window. The beach was completely black, a mixture of sand and volcanic ash, vivid testimony to Hekla's eruptions over the centuries. Large rusty barrels filled with sand were stacked in the middle of the beach, presumably to form a barrier against the breaking waves. A strong wind was blowing, bending the tall grasses that grew in tufts at the edge of the muddy tracks. The silence of the lava fields had been replaced by the powerful roar of the North Atlantic.

"You coming?"

Allen was smiling at me.

"I'm not going to stay in the car all by myself," I muttered. When I opened the door it flew out of my hand. Damn this place! My mother and Allen walked briskly alongside the ocean. I plodded behind them, hood up, hands in pockets. Stumbling over something, I looked down and saw a dead bird. Dozens of small corpses littering the beach. Nice.

Black Beach (if that, in fact, was where we were) did not resemble the Italian beaches from my childhood. True, it was autumn. Maybe the beach looked more appealing in June or July, though I couldn't imagine hordes of people cavorting on the ashy sand even then. *Starkly beautiful* was probably how the guidebooks described it, but I was in no mood to take in the scenery. From the corner of my eye I saw Allen going off by himself, leaning over to pick up shells, more shells to add to his already sizable collection. My mother was heading back, in her energetic stride, and brandishing an object, maybe an obscure plant found only in northern latitudes. I cupped my hands around my mouth.

"Find anything?"

She shouted back. I took a step forward, and stopped.

"Allen!" I scanned the length of the beach for the familiar silhouette of my husband. "Allen!"

Maman started to run.

As it happened (since he lived to tell the tale), Allen had strolled to the far end of the beach where the cliffs sheltered him from the biting wind. An unusual-looking shell caught his attention; he bent over to pick it up and lost his balance. The wet sand was heavy, and before he could draw himself up again another crashing wave knocked him down. Not one to panic easily, he gathered up his strength and willed himself to stand, but couldn't. Where he'd fallen he lay, his desert boots soaked in mud, the pockets of his parka filling with icy water, pretty little shells strewn all around him. Bereft of his glasses, he could barely make out the outline of the barrels in the distance. His legs were partially submerged; numbness had begun to invade his lower limbs.

Maman was the first one to spot him.

"Here! Quick!"

Fighting against the pull of the ocean, we dragged him away from the water. I sobbed and cursed all at once while Maman got down to business. Allen was breathing, that was the main thing. We stood him up as best we could and positioned his arms around our shoulders for support.

As the odd procession inched forward, rain started to fall.

"Shit!"

In the car Allen, teeth chattering with cold, stripped to his underpants and muffled himself up in an old plaid blanket left in the trunk for just such purposes. I turned on the ignition.

The rain was coming down in buckets.

"Can't *wait* to get the hell out of here."

I glanced at Allen shivering in the back and felt little compassion. "And don't ask me to give you my sweater."

"I don't want your sweater," he snapped.

My mother took off her coat and handed it to her son-in-law.

"No, no, it's okay."

"Take it, please."

"Thank you." He curled up under the furry wrap.

No other words were spoken until we approached Selfoss. The car suddenly hit a large pothole, causing Allen to stir.

"How do you feel?" Maman asked him.

"Much better. It's nice and warm in here."

"What a quick recovery!"

"Do you realize you almost died out there?" I asked, still seething.

"I wouldn't go that far."

"Oh yes, you would have, one more wave and goodbye Charlie."

"What do you want me to do?"

"Just admit it was a *stupid* idea to go there! I knew something horrible would happen, but you didn't listen, did you, and now look at the mess we're in. You'll catch pneumonia and God only knows when we'll get home, *if* we make it home in this *stupid* weather."

Maman started to say something. Allen put his hand on her shoulder.

"It's okay. Let her have her say."

The humming of the Volkswagen, faithfully bringing its passengers nearer to the American base, was the only reply.

Back at the house Allen ran a hot bath into which he sank gratefully. I made a large pot of tea, arranged some cookies on a plate, and started to unwind.

"What would you have done," my mother asked Allen the next day, "if things hadn't been resolved between you two last night?"

"I would have apologized to Mona, because I didn't have the right to project my anxiety onto her."

What could I say? Allen had once again surprised me with his generosity of spirit and his ability, even in the worst of circumstances, to assess a situation objectively.

After Maman left I worked for several months as a procurement order clerk in the merchandising office of the PX. My task was to order uniforms for Navy personnel. I learned to use the keypunch and to take inventory, and thrived at my grey, standard-issue desk, surrounded by cheerful, informal Americans. (Oh, how I missed the States!)

Allen and I had decided that we wouldn't remain in Iceland a third year if no transfer came through. Instead, we would move back to Philadelphia and reacquaint ourselves with good old America.

And so goodbye wind, goodbye lunar landscapes, mud pools, northern lights!

Goodbye *kronur, pylsur, fiskur, fjördur!*

Goodbye darkness, hello USA!

Chapter Eight: USA

*P*hiladelphia Revisited. We move in with my in-laws. Allen gets a job. We buy a car. We find an apartment. I get a job. It's a long commute. At the end of the school year we move closer to my work. Allen finds a new job.

*   *   *

I was hired as a freelance translator by the head librarian, Nancy, and immediately basked in the literate atmosphere of the Franklin Mint's library, staffed solely with engaging, intelligent women. It was the ideal setup: I enjoyed full administrative support while retaining the flexibility of an independent contractor. Glad to be able to practice my languages, I often called Cousteau's Oceanographic Institute in Monaco, which worked in close conjunction with the Mint on philatelic covers. Whenever foreign dignitaries visited corporate headquarters, I was called upon to interpret. I convinced my boss that the library could use more foreign language reference materials, and took the train up to New York to purchase books and dictionaries from the Librairie de France at Rockefeller Center.

Allen and I rented an apartment in bucolic Goshen, part of a sprawling, beautifully landscaped complex that included tennis courts and an outdoor pool. We drove a peppy Honda Civic, the epitome of fuel efficiency in the aftermath of the oil crisis, which drew stares from drivers of large American cars. At red lights they'd roll down their windows and ask, "How many miles do you get in this thing?" When having a second car became a necessity, Allen, who had no interest in sports cars, indulged me and bought a used MGB convertible, a jewel of a car plagued only by a leak in the soft-top when it rained. I loved flashing my beams at other MG drivers to signal adherence to an anointed group of car enthusiasts.

Yes, life was good. In fact, from a material standpoint, it was the best we had ever had.

My parents came to visit on their way back from a symposium out west. In the years since I left home, I had never played host to my father. And this would be only his second time meeting Allen.

We prepared for their arrival by scrubbing the place clean (let it not be said that we were slobs) and selecting a few simple, foolproof menus, such as steak, baked potatoes and salad. The only sour note came from the neighbor two floors down from us, a boorish woman who was in the habit of playing—banging, really—her drums at all hours, and who replied, "It's my apartment, I can do whatever I want" when I asked her, as politely as I could, to curb her musical enthusiasm.

As soon as we returned from the airport, Allen and I headed for the kitchen to prepare lunch. Papa was as charming as could be. Was this the same man who had spoken so rudely to my husband in Berne? Allen offered his father-in-law wine, making idle chatter about its provenance. Papa beamed with pleasure: good wine, good meal.

That Saturday, we all crammed into the Civic and drove to the Chesapeake Bay, weaving our way through Maryland's Eastern Shore, and stopping for lunch at a local restaurant advertising the region's famed soft-shelled crabs.

Allen's parents invited us to an early Sunday dinner at their house. As my father stepped into their living room, I worried that he might find something, or someone, not to his liking. But he didn't embarrass me, or Allen for that matter. Helen, who kept a kosher kitchen, had outdone herself: chopped liver, gefilte fish, two types of meat with vegetables, potato latkes, a tossed salad, rolls and butter, pies and cookies for dessert, among them ruggelach (small pastries made with cream cheese dough and filled with apricot preserves, walnuts, chocolate, or cinnamon). After the meal we sank into the deep, comfortable sofa to digest our food. I prayed that Harry wouldn't turn on the television, which he always did, and which always put him to sleep. But on that occasion, he merely leaned back in his La-Z-Boy and smiled contentedly.

Life continued, placid, predictable.

By spring I had become restless. Allen reapplied to DOD and received an offer to go to Malta. I was all fired up at the prospect of living in the sun-drenched Mediterranean of my youth.

"It's an island," Allen pointed out.
"I know, but it's a *warm* island."
"It's still an island, a very *small* island."
"But it's near Italy!"
"Do you remember how we got island fever in Iceland?"
"That's different. Iceland was miserable. Malta is beautiful, people go there on vacation."

In the end, Allen convinced me to hold out for a more desirable destination.

"What if there is no other offer?"
"We wait another year."

Some time in 1980 my brother got a research fellowship at the Salk Institute in California, where he moved with his wife and two children. Now we had an excuse to visit the Golden State. We flew into Los Angeles and drove down the Pacific Coast Highway in a sporty Datsun 280Z, a complimentary upgrade from the car rental company.

My brother and his family lived in a house in Del Mar with, alas, no ocean view. Nevertheless, California was intoxicating. From Del Mar—where I bought fresh croissants and pastries at a Danish *pâtisserie* on Camino del Mar every morning—it was only a short drive past the Torrey Pines State Reserve to the breathtaking Salk Institute in La Jolla, a masterpiece of modern architecture overlooking the Pacific Ocean. During the week Allen and I took my nephews, aged six and seven, on fun outings in and around San Diego: the famous Zoo with its droll gondolas; the Wild Animal Park near Escondido, where we took a safari train ride across a landscape recalling African plains, with giraffes, elephants and lions roaming around freely; the stately Hotel del Coronado and, across the bay, the Cabrillo National Monument. To the boys' utter delight, we spent an entire day at Disneyland in Anaheim. In downtown La Jolla, we admired the upscale shops on Prospect Street and took pictures of scenic La Jolla Cove, nestled among the jagged cliffs. We ate sandwiches stuffed with avocado and alfalfa sprouts, and savored Mexican specialties: quesadillas, tacos, burritos.

That summer Allen received notification from DOD that a position was available in Belgium. Belgium! Even though the assignment said SHAPE, not Brussels, it was still Belgium. We quit our jobs, sold the MG, packed up and flew the coop.

Chapter Nine: BELGIUM

DOD put us up in a hotel in Casteau where lower-echelon military personnel and civilians in transit stayed. As hotels go, this one wasn't particularly nice, not the sort of place you look forward to coming back to at the end of a house-hunting day. Nor could I linger there while Allen was at work: the cleaning crew, irritated at finding me in the room most mornings, made it clear that I was in the way. Without a car—our household shipment not due for another month—I felt stranded. And the overcast sky didn't help.

The real estate agent showed us a meager selection of unfurnished apartments in Mons, in the province of Hainaut, some forty miles southwest of Brussels. As the days dragged on with no offerings in sight, the idea of living in the country grew more and more appealing.

In Brugelette (why it was called Little Bruges I'll never know, for it bore no resemblance to the Venice of the North) we saw a brand-new *maisonnette*, a simple house on one floor, made of stone. I liked the attached garage with gravel parking space up front, the big backyard. That house was the pride and joy of the Italian mason who had built it with his own hands. But he couldn't afford to live in it, so he had decided to rent it, preferably to Americans.

We closed the deal.

Our furniture came. Since the house was completely bare, lacking even a phone outlet, we had to purchase numerous items: light fixtures, curtains, a wardrobe, a dresser, a washer/dryer. Most of my days were spent running errands: getting supplies at the PX on Route d'Ath; shopping in Mons; driving back and forth to SHAPE, about half an hour away, to mail letters at the American Post Office, or bank at the Credit Union, or fill out forms at Motor Vehicle Registration. Everywhere on base I saw soldiers and officers walking from building to building with a purpose, doing their job.

I felt out of sorts.

First, there was the matter of the house. The tiled floor was so cold to the feet that we could never get warm, even after we bought rugs and lit chimney fires. And because of the damp climate, the second bedroom became mildewed. Nothing could take the dankness out of that place.

Second, we had landed in the sticks. Somewhere between Mons and Ath, two small towns in the Borinage district, an area known for its coal mines, which were now closed but still accounted for the dreary landscape. Although I went up to Brussels on occasion, I couldn't seem to recapture the glorious days of '73-'74.

Third, I had no job prospects.

So I watched sitcoms and old American movies on TV. I moseyed around Mons, glad to have discovered, at least, an excellent *pâtisserie-confiserie* in the center of town. I cooked, I cleaned, I fiddled about.

One day Allen mentioned in passing that, when the time came, he would raise his children in the Jewish faith. The whole notion of having children scared the wits out of me. But most of all, I was surprised to hear Allen, who had never gone to synagogue during the course of our marriage, speak with such fervor about being Jewish.

By January I had come to a decision.

"I want to go back to law school."

Allen, well aware of my disenchantment, was all in favor. Researching the entrance requirements at the Université Libre de Bruxelles filled me with renewed enthusiasm and the certainty that law school would bring back a sense of purpose.

It took several trips to the Avenue Franklin Roosevelt, where the ULB campus was located, and many more phone calls. Admissions referred me to the School of Law, which referred me to the Dean's office, which referred me back to Admissions. In the end, the most significant bit of information would be a number: five. Five long years to become a lawyer. That sounded excessive. Then there were the many unanswerable questions. Assuming I got the degree, what kind of law would I be able to practice in Belgium as a non-citizen? What if I wished to practice outside Belgium, say in the US, or Switzerland? How useful would a law degree from a Belgian university really be?

Maybe I should study in Switzerland. As a Swiss citizen I'd be able to practice law without restrictions. I decided to inquire, discreetly, about the length of study at the University of Geneva. I knew that getting accepted wouldn't be a problem, but how would Allen react?

Allen nodded his approval. He understood my frustration, he said, and if I could get a law degree from Geneva in just three years, he would support me.

"Would you consider moving to Geneva?" I asked.

"Not at this point. As you know, I have a commitment to DOD. I have to stay here for at least two years."

We talked about the logistics of being in a commuter marriage and only seeing each other on holidays. Financing my studies. Finding a place to live in Geneva. Telling our parents. *Not* telling our friends.

At SHAPE our circle of acquaintances, rather than friends, included teachers and their spouses. One couple, parents of a newborn baby, rented an unusual apartment, part of a century-old, tastefully renovated *manoir* that featured several types of accommodations, some in converted barns, on a huge property with horses. They had just spent Christmas at the Club Med in Zinal, in the Val d'Anniviers, the very same valley where my parents had their chalet. As they described the alpine resort covered in powdery snow, I thought longingly of winters spent in St. Luc. I hadn't skied since Allen and I met, and missed it.

Others lived in charming country cottages, much different from our cold and damp *maisonnette,* where we were stuck until the end of the lease.

Unless I moved to Geneva.

But we weren't going to tell people about our little arrangement. Not yet, anyway. We sat at gatherings and acted as if our lives were as conventional as theirs. I wanted to shout, *I'm going to Geneva to finish law school! Isn't it great?* When I thought about the future, it was with exhilaration. Instinctively, though, I knew to keep my ebullience in check for Allen's sake. Granted, he had voiced his full support, but what if he changed his mind?

In March I went to Berne to visit my parents. Allen saw me off at the tiny Brugelette train station at dawn. It was cold and grey, and I was glad to leave the glumness of Hainaut. In Mons I changed trains, and at Brussels' Gare du Nord switched again, taking the TransEuropExpress via Luxembourg and Strasbourg to Basel. I arrived in Berne some twelve hours later, excited to be back home.

When I told my parents the news, Papa said:

"It'll be good to have a lawyer in the family."

I had expected shocked expressions, or at the very least, mild disapproval.

During the visit, my father announced that he would give me a sum equivalent to what he had already given my brother to renovate his house, as an advance on the inheritance. "That's only fair," he added. I couldn't believe my luck. Now I'd be able to pay for the move and all my expenses. This had to be a sign, a sign that what I was about to do was the right thing. The next morning Papa and I stopped by the bank to sign papers authorizing the transfer.

An offer to teach at the SHAPE Language Center came through. For two months I taught English to Italian kids, the offspring of military personnel stationed on base. There were about twenty of them, ranging from ages seven to fifteen, and we met twice a week.

I was unsure about accepting this assignment. Allen saw it as an opportunity to find out if I liked teaching, and to make contacts at the LC. I wondered if committing to any kind of employment—by now we both knew I'd be leaving for Geneva in the summer—made sense.

The first day of class I showed up with a bad case of the butterflies and begged the head of the school to find another instructor. She spent quite a bit of time reassuring me, until I finally agreed to give it a shot. We marched down that hallway, and as soon as I crossed the threshold and gazed at my flesh-and-blood pupils, my fears dissipated. These were, after all, only kids. And I knew English far better than they did. Things proceeded smoothly from that point on. I liked the interaction with the children, one of whom, an older boy, developed a crush on me. He tried to get my attention by constantly raising his hand, sometimes to give the answer, more often to ask questions, all sorts of questions. Still, I could never entirely shake the feeling that I was a fraud for teaching a language other than my own.

With the money my parents had given me I bought a car in Brussels, another Civic, exact replica of the one we owned except for the color, white with light blue interior. In June I drove to Geneva, via the Ardennes and Alsace, to find an apartment. I stayed at a *pension de famille* in a lakeside village on the outskirts of town, then moved to a centrally located hotel on Avenue de Frontenex. A realtor took me around the city, but nothing I saw inspired me. It was either too old, dirty (yes, there is dirt in Switzerland, only not on the streets), or far from the university. I was beginning to lose hope when a furnished studio in an elegant building at Crêts-de-Champel came on the market. The flat had built-in closets and a living room with garden view. One wall was taken up by floor-to-ceiling windows, which bathed the studio in sunlight. A wine-colored velvet couch and matching armchair faced a rectangular, glass-topped coffee table. Acting as a divider between the queen-size bed in one corner and the rest of the living space stood a two-sided metal bookshelf. Everything was clean, functional, pleasing to the eye. I immediately signed the lease.

LEAVING EUROPE

On the long drive back to Belgium, I had time to think. A whirlwind of events was taking me from Brugelette, where my husband resided, to Geneva, where life as a law student awaited me. While I rejoiced at the opportunity, I was also torn by it. Neither Allen nor I had ever mentioned splitting up; we looked at this arrangement as practical, temporary, consensual. Yet our life as a couple would change drastically with us living five hundred miles apart, even if we factored in holiday visits.

I returned to Brugelette and resumed *la vie conjugale* with Allen. To all appearances, we were a perfectly normal couple. Inwardly, there was unease, anxiety, guilt—not that we discussed any of those feelings. We lived side by side, day by day, talking about this and that, innocuous stuff. We didn't have any overt conflicts, no heated arguments. We merely existed, or rather, coexisted. At the same time, Allen was becoming less playful in public. His favorite little performance in the past had been to link his arm in mine, and lead me into a lively *pas de deux* to the tune of "Follow the Yellow-Brick Road" from *The Wizard of Oz* (to personalize it, he changed the pronoun in the first and last verses to *we*):

> *We're* (pausing for effect) *off to see the Wizard, the Wonderful Wizard of Oz*
> *You'll find he is a Whiz of a Wiz if ever a Wiz there was*
> *If ever, oh ever, a Wiz there was the Wizard of Oz is one because*
> *Because, because, because, because, because*
> *Because of the wonderful things he does*
> *We're . . . off to see the Wizard, the Wonderful Wizard of Oz*

Now that we each had our own car, we spent less time together. No more wisecracks about the Belgian housewives fretfully sweeping the sidewalk in front of their houses every morning. No more recap of the day's events during the ride home. No more joint trips to the open-air market in Mons. I was readying myself for the move, and Allen—well, I don't know what Allen was thinking. He carried on as before, smiling at me, cleaning the bathroom on Saturday mornings, mowing the lawn, forever being helpful. Which didn't help one bit. Had he been vile or opposed to my going to school in another country, things would have come to a head.

But Allen was being Allen: kind, patient, agreeable to whatever I proposed.

Until the eve of my scheduled departure. The Honda was already packed with my two red suitcases, odds and ends in boxes and plastic bags. It was Sunday. I was doing one last load of laundry. Allen, standing in the kitchen, grabbed my wrist as I went by.

"Don't go."

"It's too late," I said. "I'm all packed."

He gazed at me, held my wrist for several seconds, and let it drop.

I walked away. He's going to make it hard for me to go, I thought. I resisted the urge to say, *Screw it*, unload the car and curl up in my husband's arms. My body—craving the physical and emotional comfort that I knew Allen would provide—wanted to stay, but my mind was made up. If I didn't leave tomorrow, I would never leave. It had taken me months to convince myself that this was the right decision. Allen had gone along with it, and now—now . . . .

At dinner that evening we hardly spoke.

I had a fitful sleep, tossing and turning all night, revisiting my decision. Early next morning I finished loading up the car while Allen dressed for work. We said goodbye, hugging each other briefly. He drove off, skidding over the gravel. I went back into the house, sat on the bed and cried my heart out. And then, lest my resolve should crumble, I picked up my keys, locked the front door, and without a backward glance, left Brugelette.

Chapter Ten: SWITZERLAND

Classes at the University of Geneva started in October. Even though I was older (one month shy of thirty) than most other students, I relished being back in the halls of academia. I bought books, notepads, pens, and absorbed my teachers' words with the eagerness of a first-grader. University buildings were scattered around Rue de Candolle, Cours des Bastions, Plainpalais, and the aptly named Boulevard des Philosophes. Sometimes I drove the short distance from my flat in Champel, but most days I relied on public transportation.

Scenic Geneva, on the banks of Lac Léman between the Jura and the Alps, was a source of constant enchantment: the UN's stately Palais des Nations; grand hotels on Quai du Mont-Blanc; the famed Rue du Rhône jewelers; inviting cafés at Place du Molard; trendy boutiques on Rue du Marché; medieval alleys leading up to Cathédrale St-Pierre; shimmering sailboats on the green-blue water. This cosmopolitan city, not unlike Brussels, teemed with foreigners of every ilk: diplomats, civil servants, deposed monarchs, exiled despots.

I loved my calm, residential *quartier*. Contrary to popular belief, not all neighborhoods were created equal in Geneva—or the rest of Switzerland, for that matter. Les Grottes and Les Pâquis, the so-called ethnic neighborhoods, were a tad scruffy. In Les Pâquis, known for its strip clubs and assortment of colorful characters, passing prostitutes on the sidewalk in the morning—some on their way to Migros to buy groceries, others going home after a long night's work—was commonplace, and more endearing than sordid in broad daylight.

Focused on the task at hand I attended class every day, read assigned sections of the penal code, tried to master the intricacies of contract law. I wasn't particularly keen on making friends, which was just as well because I had noticed how cliquish the local students were. Should the spirit move me, I would seek out outsiders like me. What was I, anyway? Swiss? Hardly. American? Not entirely. A stranger looking in, perhaps, eternal tourist in disguise.

Allen came down for Christmas. When I saw him behind the glass partition at Cointrin, waving at me and dancing his little dance in the baggage claim area, I thought, *Just like old times.* Sweet reunion, after a three-month separation. We had arranged to visit my parents in St. Luc during the holiday; I had insisted that we book a hotel room in the village rather than stay at the chalet, where the rooms were small and the walls thin. Maman voiced her disappointment, but Papa seemed to understand our need for privacy. We spent a few restful days there, having breakfast at the Hotel Beausite and dinner at the chalet. We took leisurely walks in the picturesque village; wandered up to Chandolin, enjoying a panoramic view of the mountains around us; hiked to Ayer, where we arrived, starved, after the kitchen at the only restaurant had closed, and begged the waitress to bring us something, *anything* to eat (she produced bread and cheese). One morning we went cross-country skiing in Zinal, Allen's first venture on skis. On our way back to the ski rental shop, he hurt his thumb on a wooden gate and cried out in pain. Concerned, I asked if it was bleeding, and was puzzled when he abruptly turned away.

"I don't need your sympathy."

We ambled over to a restaurant crowded with skiers. I looked around at the twenty-somethings laughing and carrying on as twenty-somethings are wont to do, and contrasted their joviality with the awkward attempts at small talk at our table.

The vacation came to an end. At the airport, I told Allen I would visit him during February break.

But a lot happened between that conversation and February break.

First, I decided that law was not for me. The tediousness of it all! Memorizing the minutiae of each case, precedent, interpretation, exception—it was like being forced into a straitjacket, and I wanted out.

Second, I discovered jazz, serious jazz. Began to collect records, listened to them around the clock on my newly installed stereo.

Third, I entertained notions of becoming a jazz pianist. With that in mind I enrolled in an improvisation workshop at Sud des Alpes, a collective run by the AMR (Association pour la Musique de Recherche).

Fourth, I bought an electric typewriter and started a novel.

It was as if a burst of creativity had been unleashed. I cut my hair short, always a sign of new beginnings. Reclaimed my given name. Joined a fitness club in Les Pâquis. Attended jazz concerts at the New Morning. I felt alive, energetic, filled with purpose. And gradually it dawned on me that my connection to Allen was ebbing away. I called him at the high school (the house in Brugelette still didn't have a phone) one bleak day in February and told him I wouldn't be coming up to see him: I needed time to sort out my feelings—about him, us, our marriage.

* * *

February 17, 1982

Dear Mona:

After speaking with you I came home and began this letter. People were in the next room and their close proximity inhibited my responses. The things I have to say are for your ears alone.

Needless to say I am very happy that you are enthusiastically engaged in writing a book. It is a serious endeavor and one that I feel you can succeed at. Pursue it. One learns to write by writing.

I fully understand that you did not write to me. You should not feel guilty. You write to me when you want, when you feel the need to, not when you feel I need to hear from you.

You are on a rare journey of discovery. Discovering yourself. At times it may be difficult, perhaps unpleasant, but the destination is worth the expense incurred. It is your journey and you take the time necessary to complete it. I will be watching and wishing you the best always. Unfortunately for me I will not accompany you nor share in the excitement, but that is my problem, not yours.

This Easter you make plans for yourself. My expectations for the holidays will not include you. Do not misinterpret what I have written. I would love nothing better than to spend the two weeks at Easter with you. My expectations, however, are to spend them without you. My feelings need, at the moment, clearly defined expectations. I too need time now to sort out my feelings.

There is nothing wrong with what you have done, what you are doing, or what you plan to do. But I must know clearly what I am doing. It is clear to me that we are separated. It is clear to me that our marriage is over. Our friendship, our love, no. Our marriage, yes. This is not said in anger. It is a statement of fact, though a difficult one for me to write.

You have been learning to live without me and now I must learn to live without you. This will not be an easy experience for me. You can help me by not coming to see me.

I know I can depend on you for assistance, as you know you can depend on me. Change is sometimes painful. The change you are experiencing is neither right nor wrong. You are evolving and that's healthy.

You are a beautiful person. I miss you. I love you. And I will learn to cope without you. You owe me nothing. Do not look back. The future, your future is ahead of you.

This summer I will begin divorce proceedings. It's inexpensive and easy in Pennsylvania. No fault divorce, as long as neither party contests it.

Send my regards to your parents.

Love, Allen

P.S. I do not expect you to answer this letter, so please do not feel compelled to do so out of courtesy.

March 9, 1982

Dear Mona:

Received your letter written Tuesday evening. Don't reproach yourself. You're doing what you think is best. Your happiness is at stake.

As much as I want to see you at Easter I must decline your invitation. Dealing with reality can be difficult but it must be dealt with. It would be devastating for me to look forward to seeing you only to find that you changed your mind. One experience like that is enough for me. By not expecting to see you, the pain of not seeing you lessens.

I have not forgotten that you are a loving and sweet person. I miss you too. But I am learning to live without you, as I must.

Please, if you haven't already done so, mail your ID card to me.

Love, Allen

March 16, 1982

Dear Mona:

Received your letter, ID card, and your sweet surprise today.

I could not imagine what was in the packages. I laughed after I opened one of them. You even went to the trouble of gift wrapping them. It was a very nice surprise and I appreciate your thoughtfulness. You're a kind, sweet, lovable girl.

It sounds like your days are full. Life can be a joy and I am very happy to read that each day is a joyful one for you. Your letter brightened my day.

You always worked very hard at your jobs, even though you didn't particularly enjoy them. When you had a task to complete you were diligent. It is one of your strong points. I am confident that not only will you complete your book, but it will be interesting reading as well.

Yes, our marriage has ended. But look at what has begun. Keep on looking ahead. Perhaps I'll see you in June, perhaps not. We will continue to write. I'll file for divorce this summer and mail you the papers to be signed.

I doubt very much if I'll get a transfer. But it really doesn't matter. Home is where you make it. I'm very happy for you. Your outlook is positive. You have your health. You're vibrating with excitement. You make me smile. Keep it up.

Love, Allen

A candle burns
A single flame
A silent light
A partner's moon

April 19, 1982

Dear Mona:

What can I say? Come up. I think it's important that we talk. We had begun talking the last time you were here. We never really finished. I was sorely disappointed that you didn't come again. I was deeply hurt by the conversation we had in February over the phone. It wasn't so much what you said as the way you said it. Your attitude particularly. I became very depressed after that conversation. I really didn't care about anything. I was gone. Sunk. I needed time to be alone. During my stay in the Canaries I reflected a lot. Then I called you when I returned.

Among the many things you said in February, one stands out: "The more things change, the more they stay the same." Since last fall there has certainly been a lot of change. And it seems that things will continue to change. For the better? Time will supply the answer.

One of the burdens in our marriage has been the frequency with which we moved. This intensified a burden of yours: pursuing a career. So you went to Geneva. And so you continue your quest for a career, as you should. Are your chances better in Geneva? Perhaps. I want you to have all the successes that you seek. Can I be of assistance? Maybe. What is the answer? What is the question? And so the cycle becomes complete. Seeking the answer leads to the question. Unfortunately, I don't have the answer. But I do have lots of questions. Will they be of help? I don't know.

So why then should you come up? Because I ask you? Because I love you? Because I care for you? Because . . . . No. None of these is the reason. There are no reasons. Then what is the point of this letter? The point is that you are free to choose. You don't have to do anything. You are independent, relying upon your own resources. Whatever your choice I will support it. Whatever your decision I *will continue to love you. I'm not angry with you now and I will not be angry with you in the future.*

But what about you? How do you feel about you? Be fair to yourself. Make your goals reachable.

Love, Allen

P.S. Don't be stubborn.

* * *

At the New Morning one evening I heard the Stan Getz Quartet. The tenor saxophonist, in fine form, cajoled the audience with his lyrical instrument. The club was packed. I swayed to the beat of the music. The sidemen—pianist, bass player, drummer—were in complete sync. I admired the ease with which they performed riffs, broke into a solo, joined in again—all the things I struggled with in my jazz improv class. After a while I was drawn to the delicate, precise playing of the drummer. No matter how far I leaned over in my seat, the drummer's face remained hidden behind the cymbals. I became mesmerized by his hands. Up until then I hadn't paid drummers much attention: they were part of the rhythm section. But on that occasion, the invisible drummer's technique took on an entirely new meaning. What would a jazz combo be without the drums? Not only was the drummer a key member of the group, he was the glue, the binding force behind the band.

I had to see his face. After the final set he stood up, smiling, and I knew what to do.

We spoke. He was charming. I invited him to get a bite. He admitted to being hungry, but first he needed to pack away his drums (the unglamorous part of the show, he called it). At the club I had run into a classmate from law school, a nerdy type who followed me around like a little dog. While I spoke to the drummer he stood right next to me, asking all sorts of questions that the musician answered graciously. I wanted the student to disappear in the worst way—he was cramping my style, maybe even giving the impression that we were a couple. But I couldn't shake him off without appearing rude. He tagged along, talking non-stop, while I searched for a restaurant that might still be open. That's when Puppy Dog came to the rescue.

"You can come to my flat!"

The drummer and I looked at each other.

"I'll make spaghetti. I make pretty good spaghetti."

After a moment's hesitation, we agreed that it was indeed an excellent idea.

The student lived in modest digs on the top floor of an old building. It was your typical *mansarde*, the kind that Mimi of *La Bohème* fame might have inhabited: a single room with a sink and hot plate in one corner where our host prepared a very large pot of spaghetti. We talked until the early morning hours. When Puppy Dog vanished to the bathroom down the hall, the drummer asked if he was my boyfriend.

"God, no!"

And then, because that sounded mean, I added:

"Just someone I know from school."

Shortly after that exchange, the drummer and I thanked the student and left together.

It was late, it was cold. I opened my car door.

"Do you want to come over to my place?"

"Sure."

We sped through the deserted streets.

I wasn't destined to become a jazz pianist. First, I found it hard to discard the rigid mantel of years of classical training. It was one thing to change a few notes here and there when you played Ravel or Gerhswin, quite another to actually improvise. Following sheet music was so much easier than coming up with original riffs and licks! And second, wasn't I a bit old to be *starting off* as a jazz musician?

But—and there always was a "but" in those soliloquies—if I couldn't make it as a jazz musician, maybe I could make it as a photographer of jazz greats. In order to do that, I needed equipment. The photographer who sold me the goodies—Nikon FM2 with 28mm, 85mm, 180mm and 70-210mm lenses, filters, flash, tripod, leather case for lugging everything around—spent a long time advising me, and finally recommended I attend one of his workshops. In a basement studio a small group of us shutterbugs learned how to develop our own black-and-white photos. During the day I roamed the city to hone my skills, taking close-ups of flowers in the Jardin Botanique, shots of the Jet d'Eau from different angles, steamboats on Lake Geneva, sunsets, monuments, children at play in the Parc des Eaux-Vives.

At the end of the workshop the instructor took me aside and asked if he could take my portrait. I agreed to sit for him, only to find out that what he had in mind was not simple portraiture. "You're so striking," he kept saying as he clicked away, inches from my face, "almost androgynous."

At last I jumped off the stool. He protested. I left him there with his tongue hanging out.

In those days my bathroom doubled as a darkroom, while in the living room films hung out to dry with plastic laundry pegs, like Italian laundry, on a string secured by shelves at one end and picture hooks at the other. My little kingdom, my lab, consisted of a small folding table I set up over the toilet, giving me easy access to running water from the sink. I had enough room for three or four rectangular tanks filled with various solutions (developer, stop bath, fixer, rinse), as well as the necessary tools of the trade (tongs, measuring cups, thermometer, timer, etc.). When there were concerts at the New Morning I brought along my camera and discreetly took aim at the musicians on stage. I saw other photographers, those affiliated with the news media, moving about to obtain that unique shot in a way that was both disruptive to the audience and, so I imagined, annoying to the performers. I swore I would never become one of those obnoxious, self-important types. My specialty would be to take great photographs of jazz artists without being noticed.

And what a cast passed through Geneva! Art Blakey and the Jazz Messengers; Max Roach; Johnny Griffin; Elvin Jones and the Jazz Machine; McCoy Tyner; David Murray; Steve Coleman; Sun Ra and his Arkestra; Olu Dara; Henry Threadgill; Pharoah Sanders; Billy Hart; George Russell Big Band. At the same time, my LP collection was growing. First I tried to get hold of every album that featured Victor, my drummer and inspiration. Then on to the legends: Miles, Coltrane, Bird, Monk, Ella, Dizzy, Mingus, Basie, Duke, Dexter, Oscar, Erroll. In the process I discovered Keith Jarrett, Wayne Shorter, Ron Carter, Eddie Lockjaw Davis, Herbie Hancock, Clifford Brown, Freddie Hubbard, Roy Eldridge, Cannonball Adderley, the Modern Jazz Quartet, Ornette Coleman, Yuseef Lateef, Rahsaan Roland Kirk, Archie Shepp, David Sanborn, Carla Bley, Jaco Pastorius, Hubert Laws, Stéphane Grappelli, Muhal Richard Abrams, Chick Corea. Especially loved Lee Morgan's trumpet in *Night of the Cookers*, and couldn't get enough of Les McCann's "Compared to What" on the *Swiss Movement—Live at Montreux* album.

Soaked up the sounds at record speed, all because of Victor.

* * *

April 25, 1982

Dear Mona:

Just received your letter. After the third reading I was able to decipher all words save for two.

First, let me assure you that I will not contest a divorce. I respect your decision and will abide by it. I understand your concern regarding the length of time it takes to complete divorce proceedings. It is only natural that you want to bring a legal end to our marriage as quickly as possible. In this we are in complete agreement. Nevertheless, I would appreciate the opportunity to see what it would cost for a lawyer, etc. in Phila. I suspect that not only will it be cheaper, but it will take less time as well. If I'm proven wrong I will, of course, be happy to share the costs with you. If not, I will go ahead and file for divorce this summer. In any event I will do nothing to hinder the paperwork that has evidently started.

It's good to read that you are exercising on a regular basis. I am too. Once a routine is developed it becomes easier to adhere to it.

Let me also congratulate you on getting a job. Sounds good and I wish you a long and fruitful career.

We are friends. As friends I hope we keep in contact. If the truth be known, you have made a wise choice.

Love, Allen

P.S. Relax.

May 7, 1982

Dear Mona:

Just received your letter, SHAPE plates, etc. Thank heavens for your typewriter.

As I read about Mr. Peel I shook my head with disbelief. I am very happy that you did not retain him. From what you wrote it seems you would have nothing but trouble from him. Do you think you are going to have difficulties from me? Do you? Has it crossed your mind? Once? Just for a moment? I hope not. But that is a subjective hope. In any case, you really have nothing to be concerned about. I have no intention of doing anything that will delay our divorce. I will keep you informed, fully, of everything that transpires. You can trust me. But that is my subjective opinion. Can you really trust me? What do your friends think? They can be more objective than me. Relax. I have not changed that much, Mona. You can trust me. Why? Because I say so? Yes. It's as simple as that. It's all so very simple.

My mother is presently gathering information regarding divorce proceedings in Pennsylvania. She hasn't written back to date. As soon as she does I will forward the information to you. If I can begin any paperwork before I depart, I will. Otherwise I will have all paperwork completed this summer. I will be seeking a No Fault Divorce. I am and you are a resident of Pennsylvania. So please be patient. I am not hiding anything from you. I have no hidden agenda. I seek no revenge. I am not angry. I love you. I want the best for you. Is that bullshit? Frankly I don't care what it is. These are my feelings towards you: love and concern. All very simple. So uncomplicated. Love and concern. And we will be getting a divorce. Even though the courts may be moving slowly in the summer. Tell your friends what I have written and get an *objective point of view. For, objectively, I may be a real dyed-in-the-wool bastard. You just keep on doing what you feel is best. Don't ask me. Tell me. Do you still trust me? I guess it really doesn't matter. You can trust yourself. I trust you.*

I don't think it was wise to send your passport back. Even after it expires I suspect you could use it to get a new passport from the US Embassy. But it's your choice. If you want it back let me know. Talk it over with a friend. Be objective.

Now, about the "wise choice." What did I mean? I was leading you down a dead-end street. As long as you were with me, you were a second class citizen. You were a follower. Worse still, I was dragging you down and suffocating you. And if the truth be known, I was a bore. But that's all history. You've made your decision and it's full steam ahead. In your heart you know it's right. Nothing to discuss. It's over. What can I say? The more things change, the more they stay the same. Fact or opinion? At this point what's the difference?

You have your independence. You have your job. You have your apartment. You have your car. You have your skis. You have Geneva. You have your exercise (keep it up). You have your laundry (and not mine). You're such a tushie. So I miss you. I love you. I'll divorce you. Am I tense? Relax. Everything is okay. Do you trust me? Do you? Not to worry. Well, have got to do the dishes. How mundane.

Love, Allen

P.S. Intended to mail this letter on Friday. But! Before I knew it the day was over and I still did not get to the post office. So I will take this opportunity to share a few thoughts. I am not opposed to getting a divorce. If you will be happier divorced, then no other arguments need to be presented. This question has been gnawing at me: Will you, in fact, be happier divorced? I don't know. More important: do you? If you feel that your love for me has changed in a way that would make you unhappy to live with me, then certainly a divorce is necessary. I don't know if this is the case. Of course it's really not important that I know as it is that you know. Well, enough of what I don't know. Let me share with you some things I do know.

I do know that you are an important part of my life. I knew this before you left. But your importance to my life is much greater than I had previously thought. The entire period of your absence has been a difficult one for me. It has torn me up and there are many jagged edges. But this is my problem. What I'm trying to say is this: you gave me more than you took. You were a wealthy partner and you were generous. Money can buy a lot of things. But many intangibles money just cannot buy. We were rich when we had the least amount of money. We grew poorer as we gained more dollars. And now we are broke. Bankrupt. Yes, you are correct. It's over, as it should be. Our priorities need to be looked at anew. A reorganization is necessary. A new start.

If you still love me, I ask you, Mona, to join with me on our new start. If you do not love me, then our new start will be a lonely one for me. In any event we will, we are, starting over. I have learned much during the past several months. Some lessons were more difficult than others. Mistakes have been made. Errors in judgment. But there is nothing wrong with making a mistake as long as you learn from it. And with the knowledge gained, not repeat the same error. And that is the crux of the matter. Was your marriage to me a mistake? If it was, certainly you do not want to repeat it. If it was not, then I think the prospects for a happy life together are good. In either case, I still feel that it is important that we see each other. If you don't want to come here I can come to Switzerland.

Danger: Long letter—may be hazardous to your health.

* * *

My marriage to Allen was over. Now that I knew, I wanted a quick divorce, which is why I'd gone to see an American lawyer in Geneva about filing in Switzerland. But Mr. Peel was full of bad news: the entire process could take a year, it would be costly, and no-fault divorce wasn't an option under Swiss law. The worst part was the way he kept leering at me, even suggesting dinner.

I enjoyed life in Geneva. In the winter I went skiing in Haute-Savoie, less than an hour away on the Autoroute Blanche. In the warmer weather there was swimming and sunbathing at the Bains des Pâquis. I saw plays at the Grand Théâtre, and went to classical concerts at Victoria Hall where I sat enthralled by the prowess of my idol, Martha Argerich, the fiery Argentinian pianist. (A resident of Geneva and true bohemian, Martha lived in an old, nondescript house surrounded by an overgrown garden.) I got myself a job at one of those instant photo-developing places at the train station, figuring I might as well start earning some money. Although I was proficient at developing my own pictures, I had yet to sell any. I'd show them to the performers and when they nodded their approval, I gave them away. I didn't have the makings of a businesswoman, but preferred to help struggling (as I perceived them to be) musicians with odd jobs—driving band members to and from their hotel; acting as their guide and interpreter; taking them to the Restoroute on the Geneva-Lausanne highway for late dinners.

I had told my parents about dropping out of law school, and was relieved by their sober reaction. Maman, still supportive, listened to me rave about jazz and photography, photography and jazz. One day I called her to describe a worrisome rash that had developed in my genital area, and I heard Papa shouting in the background:

"It's syphilis! She's got syphilis!"

That summer Victor, on tour with another band, reappeared for a few days. I spent every precious moment in his company, ferrying him around town for rehearsals, sharing meals, watching him play. He liked the black-and-white shots of his fellow artists, and tried to sneak a peak at my budding novel.

"Nobody gets to read it until it's finished," I said, gathering up the loose sheets.

"What is it about?"

"I can't tell you."

By now I was seriously in love. I had never fallen for a black man before. Most of the musicians I photographed at the New Morning were black Americans. Unwittingly, but not unpredictably, I had plunged into new territory—a mysterious culture, right in the heart of Calvin's city.

* * *

October 6, 1982

Dear Mona:

Enjoyed reading your letter very much. Glad to hear that your relationship with your father has evolved to the point you described in your letter. It seems he has accepted you as you are and your relationship will grow as a result.

Your trip to Berne, as you wrote, seems to have been worth the effort. It's ironic that your grandmother's final act was the bringing together of the family. A lot of love has been bundled away for many years and now, perhaps, cords are being untied and your family will begin to share that love more openly.

Sounds like you're doing a lot of exciting things, which excites me too. Would be interested in seeing a photo or two of your work.

Also glad to read that Bella contacted you. Lots of possibilities exist for two talented people in New York. Let me know if you go and what you hope to pursue.

Have been exercising on a regular basis and I'm back up to a mile a day of jogging. Definitely feel better when I exercise. Found out that I need 24 hours in Library Science to be a school librarian. Next summer I intend to take another nine credits. Thinking about taking Ed. Leave during school year '84-'85 (earliest date possible) and getting a Master's in Lib. Science.

The union, much to my surprise, is still going strong at SHAPE, even though we lost the Atlantic Region to OEA. Presently we have 22 members (that's what we ended up with last year), with possibility of picking up two or three more.

Enjoy hearing from you. Write again—soon if possible.

Love, Allen

P.S. Haven't heard anything more from the lawyer. All paperwork is in and divorce should be final sometime in November.

LEAVING EUROPE

October 20, 1982

Dear Mona:

First let me thank you for the picture. It is excellent and it gives me pleasure to gaze at it. I'm not going to bore you with the qualities that make it such a good photo. Let it suffice to say that if you have any others like that one, I would appreciate receiving them.

Glad to hear that you're in contact with Bella. If you write to her, please send my regards to her, her husband, and the children. Such excitement: New York, TV, money, etc. What do I think? I can only think that you must pursue that which makes you happy. Some things are easier to get than others. It's usually the long-term goals that present a problem. How long is a long-term goal? Six months? Six years? I don't know. No matter how long or short, the goal must be attainable. Is it a reasonable goal to pursue? Are the chances for success high? Probability for success depends on a multitude of variables, some of which may not be easy to control or not controllable at all. More important: how many of the variables can you control? Certainly the enthusiasm is there. No matter what you decide, it's important to make everything a learning experience. We easily learn from our successes and though it may be a bit more difficult, we can learn from our failures too.

Yes, it's true, I do need 24 credits to be a certified librarian. I received a B for each of the three courses I took this past summer. Nine credits down and fifteen to go. Will be taking another nine credits this summer. Yes, I'm still president of the OFT. We have 23 members to date.

Brugelette is, of course, still the same. Not sure if I told you in the last letter but I'm taking French classes two evenings a week. I'm not fluent by a long shot but a few more words are sinking in.

If you haven't already received the package that I sent, you will soon. It contains all the clothes that you left here. Couldn't bring myself to throw them out. So look through the box and you can decide what to keep and what to throw away.

When you have a chance, write.

Love, Allen

* * *

By fall I had quit my job and was thinking about moving to New York. As much as I liked Geneva, it was still a small town. New York, on the other hand, was the capital of jazz, the city that never slept, the place where anything could happen. In order to get a little closer to making it happen, I wrote to all three television networks, inquiring about employment opportunities. NBC and ABC both had the courtesy to reply—nothing at the moment, my resume would be kept on file, I should contact them once there. I could just see it now: I'd get this terrific job working in television (something behind the scenes), make lots of money, and in my spare time go to every single jazz club and continue to take pictures.

New York, with all its possibilities, was calling.

Meanwhile, my father, on the verge of retirement, was contemplating a return to the French-speaking part of the country. He and my mother had scouted the area between Lausanne and Geneva, looking for houses with a view of the lake. Papa saw a parcel of land in Cologny, a well-heeled municipality near Geneva, and he began to formulate plans to build a villa there with a local architect. One day he invited me to have lunch with him, my mother and the architect at the Auberge du Lion d'Or in Cologny. After the introductions, we sat down at a round table and made pleasant chitchat. At one point, the architect (not a bad-looking one at that) turned to me with an engaging smile.

"And what do you do in Geneva, Mademoiselle?"

Papa's reaction was swift.

"It's Madame," he corrected the architect, as if he were a naughty schoolboy, "not Mademoiselle!"

My honor—I was still, officially, married to Allen—had been saved. During the rest of the meal, the architect didn't dare make eye contact with me. I left straight after dessert, proffering excuses about a prior commitment.

My parents had been duly informed of my pending divorce. I hadn't volunteered any details, and they hadn't pried, for which I was thankful. When I announced my decision to move to New York, they didn't bat an eyelid. Perhaps, by then, they had resigned themselves to the fact that, when it came to their daughter, nothing ever seemed to turn out as planned.

* * *

November 5, 1982

Dear Mona:

Thank you for your warm birthday greeting; it is much appreciated.

Your move to New York sounds exciting. Your attitude seems good. I'm confident that you will meet with success in getting a job. You do have a lot to offer. Be patient and remain confident and you will get the kind of job you are seeking.

Yes, I received a letter from your mother and your brother upon my return from Philly. It was nice that they took the time to write and, of course, I answered their letters. Your mom and I have been exchanging letters, your brother never answered mine—which was not unexpected. In any case, your mother wrote that she would like to come up to Belgium and I told her she was welcome. I always enjoyed speaking with her, and I welcome the opportunity to see her again. As a matter of fact, I expect her to come up on the 13th.

If you sell your typewriter, please take your time when writing. I have become a bit spoiled with your typed letters.

Mona: you know I wish you the very, very best. It makes me happy to see you happy. In your letters you certainly sound happy.

Love, Allen

* * *

Bella and I remained in touch throughout the years. After her schooling in Switzerland she had returned to Ethiopia and married a man much older than herself, with whom she had two children. The family relocated to Germany and Guyana, and finally settled in Queens, in an apartment complex on Union Turnpike where a lot of United Nations families lived—Bella's husband worked as an economist at the UN—because of its proximity to the UN School. Bella was able to secure, on my behalf, a studio apartment in her building, starting December 1st.

During my last visit to my parents before moving, we went to have lunch at JC's house in Wabern, minutes away from the Roschi. While the atmosphere was convivial enough, I couldn't help but notice that during the meal my brother seemed annoyed with me. Afterwards, with everyone paying attention to the dog, the cat, the children, he and I had a few minutes alone in the garden.

"What's the matter with you?" I asked.

He denied that anything was the matter. When pressed further, he raised his arms in exasperation.

"I can't believe you! First you divorce Allen, who is a very nice guy. And now you're off to New York."

"First of all, you only met Allen twice in your life, and second of all, you don't know anything about the reasons for our divorce, which are none of your business anyway."

"You can't stick with anything."

"That's what you think, but I've got a good feeling about New York and it would be nice if you could muster up a little enthusiasm."

"I give it six months, tops. No, make that six weeks."

* * *

November 30, 1982

Dear Mona:

If all went well you should be reading this letter in New York. Did not intend for so much time to elapse since my last letter. The purpose of this letter, though, is not to provide you with excuses—it is to provide you with information.

First: I received your money order, which you know was totally unnecessary. In any event I cashed it and thank you for the gesture and the money, which I suspect you could have put to far better use.

Second: Also received your last letter telling of your impending departure for New York. My heart is with you and you know I wish you every success and much happiness.

Yes, your mother, at the last moment, decided not to come to see me after all. She gave me the same reason she gave you. She felt it better not to interfere. I wrote back that I understood and that she was always welcome. This spring I may go down to Switzerland and if I do I will, of course, stop by your parents and say hello (your brother too perhaps).

Yes, Mona, I do have faith in you. You are a very capable person with all kinds of talents. No matter what, you must never forget it and never lose faith in yourself. I'm rooting for you. Just remember, looking for a job is one of the most difficult things to do.

Good to read that you have an apartment. I think it will be better for you not to have to live with Bella. Privacy is very important. Bella and her husband will be close at hand, though, to give needed assistance. In short, your living conditions sound good.

You may find that a car is not absolutely necessary when living in New York City. The transportation system is vast and will take you wherever you need to go.

I can't imagine how you felt when that drunken idiot started banging on your door in the middle of the night. Sounds like you handled it very well. Get the police on the line and keep on calling till they come. I don't think you will encounter the same kind of problem in N.Y. If I remember correctly, there are doormen on duty all night. I don't think weapons are necessary, but a good dead bolt on your door wouldn't hurt.

I do believe you, Mona, when you write that you want me to be happy. Things have been going along nicely for me, and I am happy.

As soon as you're settled send me your address and your phone number.

Dear, dear Mona: My love is with you.

Allen